Sunset

Deck Plans

By the Editors of Sunset Books and Sunset Magazine

Ample planters provide the focal point for this two-level deck (see page 65).

Sunset Publishing Corporation ■ **Menlo Park, California**

A series of small decks links gazebo and patio, transforming a small yard into a serene and focused garden (see pages 30–31).

Book Editor
Lynne Gilberg

Research and Text
Philip Edinger
Lance Walheim

Coordinating Editor
Suzanne Normand Mathison

Design
Joe di Chiarro

Illustrations
Bill Oetinger
Mark Pechenik

Photographers
California Redwood Association: 8 top right, 9 top, 72; **Jay Graham:** 7; **Philip Harvey:** 4, 6, 8 bottom left and right, 9 bottom, 12; **Ralph Stark:** 1; **Peter O. Whiteley:** 8 top left; **Russ Widstrand:** 24; **Tom Wyatt:** 2.

Decks by Design

Sunset Books invited professional designers to submit plans for decks that homeowners can build. In this book we present the 15 designer decks that we selected—plans that solve common site problems, are easy to follow, and use space in imaginative and aesthetically satisfying ways.

To make these designs work for you, we include building plans, lists of materials needed for each deck, and detailed notes to guide you through any areas that require a little extra instruction. And we tell you how to estimate the quantities of building materials you'll need for the actual size of your own new deck.

In addition, a gallery of color photos in the opening chapter shows how decks can enhance outdoor living. You'll learn how to modify plans to suit your site and how to match your new deck to your home. We also offer a whole chapter of supplementary ideas—how to vary decking surface patterns, for example, and how to build around trees or boulders. We suggest a variety of deck "extras," from movable planters and benches to privacy screens, sun-shading overheads, and even a hidden sandbox.

For their valuable help with this book, we thank each of the designers whose plans and ideas are included; architect David Trachtenberg for advising us and checking the plans in chapter 2; Geoff Alexander for his technical review of chapter 2; Scott Atkinson for his editorial contribution; Marcia Williamson for copy editing the manuscript; Kathy Oetinger for cutting color screens for the illustrations; JoAnn Masaoka Van Atta and Lynne Tremble for photo scouting and styling; and the California Redwood Association for their assistance.

Cover: Curves and angles, changes of level, and diagonal deck lines subtly mimic the surrounding hills to create the illusion of endless space (see pages 40–42). Landscape architect: Peter Koenig. Cover design by Susan Bryant. Photography by Philip Harvey. Photo styling by JoAnn Masaoka Van Atta.

Note to Readers

Editor, Sunset Books: Elizabeth L. Hogan

Third printing December 1993

CONTENTS

GETTING STARTED

There are many great reasons to build a deck. You already know many of them or you wouldn't be thinking about building one. Chances are, like most people, you want to spend more time outdoors and you want to be comfortable once you're there. This book will help you build a new deck to accomplish that.

Constructing a deck, even with the help of professional plans, is no different from any other do-it-yourself project: your success is related to the quality of thought you give the project before you get started. And that's what this chapter is about. We begin by presenting a gallery of photos of decks that solve some of the problems you may have. We guide you through the planning process: understanding the structure of a deck; matching a deck to the style of your house; adapting plans; and building the design, step by step. Plan your deck well and it will be more attractive, more useful, more comfortable, and more cost-effective.

Built for entertaining large crowds and guarded by a copper pipe railing, the star of this elegantly planned redwood deck is the sofa in the center. The edge of the top deck forms the seat; the planter supports the back. See page 54 for plans.

DECKS THAT WORK

Below, and on the following three pages, you see eight successful decks. These decks are aesthetically pleasing, and they solve problems. Some improve the appearance of a home, some enhance a feature of a garden, all expand outdoor living space. We show these decks to inspire you as you define your needs and your goals. You can borrow ideas presented in these designs as well as in the Finishing Touches chapter to make one of the plans in Chapter Two work better for your situation.

Multiple decks cater to an active family. Cedar-shingled walls, deck skirts, planters, and sheltering arbors tie deck areas to the house. Design: Richard Schwartz, Builder.

Amidst the branches of an ancient oak, this redwood deck is a place to enjoy the woodsy outdoors. Handsomely crafted railings lend the feeling of quality furniture. Soft curves add a touch of contemporary sophistication to the back of an older home. Design: Gary Marsh, All Decked Out.

DECKS THAT WORK

Nestled in a narrow garden, a small redwood deck creates a private place for plants and people. Design: Josephine Zeitlin.

A sturdy railing topped with round finials and painted to match the house trim adds Victorian charm to elevated redwood decks. Lath conceals deck framing; color matches house siding. Circular shape and grand stairway soften the lines of the house. Design: Gordon Builders.

A rock-hugging, low-level deck on sleepers with staggered ends and a gravel base (for drainage) preserves that "ole swimmin' hole" look. Landscape architect: Ransohoff, Blanchfield, Jones, Inc.

Above a foggy valley, deck and see-through railing are built to enjoy the view. Hole in decking gives tree room to grow; 2 by 6 edging keeps it safe. Landscape architects: Royston, Hanamoto, Alley & Abey.

On a formerly unusable slope, a deck transforms a front yard into a comfortable neighborhood gathering spot. Planter box around tree well provides a place for garden color. Landscape contractor: Gary McCook.

French doors, leading to simple redwood deck and stylish Oriental garden, graciously link the inside of the house to the outdoors. The dining room feels large and open while the garden beckons you outside. Design: David Van Atta.

TAKING SOME BEARINGS

Before you choose a deck design from this book or create one of your own, you need to think carefully about what you really want that deck to do for you. The best way to do this is to go through a simplified design process and become familiar with the basics of deck construction.

Site Considerations

Deciding where you'll build your new deck is the first step in its design. This choice may seem obvious. For instance, you may know you want your new deck outside your living room. But the implications of your decision may not be as obvious as you think.

Microclimates. Ask yourself what the weather is like outside your living room. The general climate of your area—whether summers are sunny and hot or windy and cool—will determine how and when you use your deck and should influence its design. Do you need an arbor to provide shade during the hottest part of the day? Do you need a buffer to block strong winds?

On a smaller scale, the microclimates within your lot may also affect where and how you build your deck. These pockets differ from the general climate of a region because of their orientation or proximity to large physical objects such as buildings or trees.

How well you take advantage of the general climate of your area and the specific microclimates around your home will have a great deal to do with how much you enjoy your deck.

Sun and comfort. The amount and intensity of sunlight that hits your deck usually determines how comfortable you are when you use it. And since the angle of the sun changes not only hour by hour but season by season, you should think carefully about when you'll use the deck and what the weather will be like at that time of day and season of the year.

If you live in an area with hot summers and mild winters, shade may be welcome in summer, but not in winter. By thoughtfully positioning an arbor or deciduous tree, you can usually provide shade for a deck when the sun is high in the summer sky but allow sunlight through in winter, when the sun is lower.

The orientation of your house will also influence how much and when sun reaches your deck. In general, a deck on the east side of a house is sunny in the morning, while a west-facing one receives afternoon sun. South-facing decks get the

WORKING WITH MICROCLIMATES

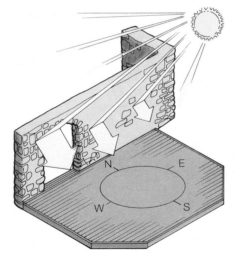

Reflected heat off a south-facing wall turns a cool deck into comfortable warm zone.

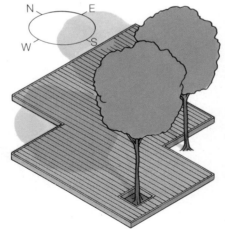

Shade trees cool a south-facing deck in summer. If deciduous, they allow warm sun through in winter.

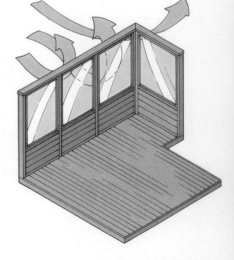

Glass or plastic panels let warm sun in while preserving view and blocking cool breezes.

most sun and are warmest year-round. Those with a northern exposure are coolest.

Where summers are cool, the heat reflected onto a deck from a south-facing wall may be just the extra warmth you need. But in a hot area, the same wall could be a glaring nightmare.

Dealing with wind. Like sunlight, wind can be both a blessing and a curse. A strong, constant breeze can make a deck feel too chilly for outdoor dining or entertaining. On the other hand, a gentle breeze can make a hot deck much more appealing.

If you live in a breezy area, your house may be your most effective windbreak. If possible, build your deck on the sheltered side of the house or design a deck that has a protected area. You might wrap an L-shaped deck around a corner of the house; which part of the deck you'd use when would then depend on whether or not the wind were blowing.

There are many ways to deal with wind (see illustration below). Usually it is best not to block the wind completely, but to redirect or buffer it.

Rain and snow. Unless you enclose your deck completely, you probably won't be using it during rain or snow. But heavy precipitation can affect a deck structurally. If you live in an area where such weather occurs, be sure that there is proper drainage underneath the deck and that gutters from the roof do not empty onto or beneath it. In an area with heavy snowfall, consult a structural engineer to be sure your deck can handle the extra weight.

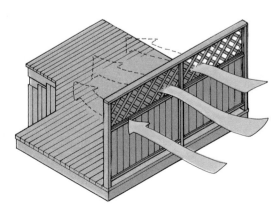

A partial screen diffuses wind without completely blocking it, providing some cooling in hot areas.

BASE PLAN

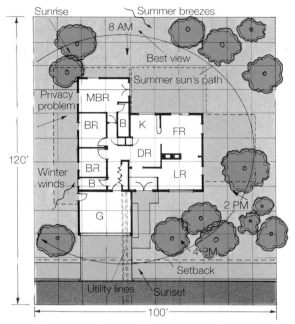

Final base plan shows all the factors that may affect potential deck locations.

The Base Plan

Once your ideas begin to develop, it's helpful to start putting them on paper. The best way to do this is to create a base plan. This preliminary plan should be drawn to scale on graph paper and include the dimensions of your lot; indicate the location of the house and other structures; and show utility lines, setbacks, existing trees and shrubs, and any objects that might affect the design. It can also reflect natural features such as views, sun and wind patterns, even circulation patterns. A sample base plan is shown above.

Make several photocopies of your base plan and use them to sketch out various deck designs.

Legal Considerations

One of the first steps in designing any deck is to check with your local building department to find out whether you need a building permit and learn what codes might affect the deck's construction. Local codes and ordinances can govern the height of a deck, the materials from which it is built, its proximity to lot lines, and certain details of its construction. If you fail to comply, you could be fined or even forced to dismantle your deck.

Also check your property deed for possible building restrictions or easements that might affect a deck's location or construction.

MATCHING YOUR NEEDS

How do you like to spend time outdoors? That could be the most important question you ask yourself when you choose among the plans in this book. The answers will help you plan a deck that meets your family's specific needs.

Entertaining. Sooner or later, almost everyone uses a deck for a party. But if you entertain often, you'll want to make sure your deck is large enough to handle groups comfortably. One way to do this is to stake out the basic size and configuration of your deck, then invite over as many friends as you usually entertain and see how well they fit in that space.

How much seating will you need? Visualize where you might place outdoor furniture. Built-in benches are easy to include if you think of them before you begin construction. Decide where to position benches to allow for easy conversation. This is best done with people arranged face to face.

Arbor-covered dining area and poolside decking is tailor-made for a family that likes to entertain outdoors. Landscape design: Peter Koenig.

For nighttime entertaining, think about outdoor lighting; it makes a deck safer and more inviting in the evening.

Dining. If you like to eat outdoors, make sure your deck is large enough to accommodate tables and chairs (a 12-foot square is usually adequate for a table and chairs to seat four). You might want to incorporate a built-in table with benches in the deck's construction. Consider how easy it will be to get from the kitchen to the deck. If a wall separates the two, adding a door or a service window could make it easier to move food outdoors.

Plan a place for a barbecue. This should be an out-of-the-way spot where no one will bump into the grill and where smoke won't be a nuisance. It's best to keep the barbecue off the decking so that falling embers don't burn the wood.

Gardening. Wooden planters can be handsomely worked into a deck design. Just be sure to allow for proper drainage. Any wood in contact with soil should be pressure-treated or decay resistant (see pages 86–87).

Deck construction often covers up hose bibbs. Move these before you begin building or install an automatic irrigation system.

Privacy. Building an elevated deck can expose as many unpleasant views as attractive ones. Try moving a ladder around and standing on it at the approximate height of your future deck. What can you see? And who can see you?

If you value privacy, or your new view is unsightly, plan to add screens, arbors, or landscaping to remedy the problem.

Storage. No matter how you will use your deck, you'll always value storage space. Where will you put the hose and other garden tools or children's play equipment? Where does the garden furniture go in bad weather? On sloping property, the most obvious place is underneath the deck where waterproof closets or shelves can be easily built, using the deck's foundation for support. Conceal such storage by "skirting" around your deck's support posts (see page 80).

You can also build lift-top benches and incorporate closets into the design of overheads.

MATCHING YOUR HOUSE

A deck should be more than just functional. When designed well, it adds beauty and character to your home, not to mention value. It should complement your house and garden, accentuating their most desirable qualities and minimizing any shortcomings.

Designers and architects use a number of devices to ensure that a deck visually complements a house. Here are some of the most useful.

Keep in scale. A large flat deck outside a small house seems out of place—more like a landing platform than an inviting outdoor living area. Likewise, a small deck off a large house feels insecure, and is seldom very useful.

One of the best ways to avoid the landing-platform syndrome is to break up a large deck into several smaller, multilevel or satellite decks. This can be particularly effective on sloping property.

Take cues from existing design. To make a new deck seem as though it has always been part of your property, repeat some of your house's features in the deck's design. For example, stain or paint the deck to match or complement the house color.

Highlighting natural features in your garden as part of a deck design can result in a stunningly beautiful outdoor environment. Don't think of large rocks, trees, streams, or rough terrain as obstacles, but as possible focal points. Weave the deck amid the rocks. Let a tree grow up through the deck's surface, and build a bench around it so you can enjoy the shade. Use multilevel decking to accentuate the handsomeness of rugged terrain.

Create smooth transitions. A deck should entice people outdoors. The only way it can is if you provide a fluid transition from the inside of your house to the outside. This will increase the amount your deck is used, and it will also open interior areas of your house to light and air, bringing the beauty of the outdoors inside.

Wide French or glass doors that open out onto a deck make the outdoors look inviting; a single door that opens to a series of steep steps does not. Consider how people will view the deck from inside the house and how they will get out to it. Sometimes simply adding a wider door or a larger window can make the indoor-outdoor relationship much more satisfactory.

Also try to create attractive transitions between different areas of the deck and between the deck and the rest of the garden. Steps should not be too steep, narrow, or intimidating. Railings should be sturdy, and look it.

Use interesting angles. If your initial designs look too blocky, try cutting off some of the sharp corners, creating octagons from squares. Doing so can make the deck itself seem more interesting and can soften the severe look of a rectilinear house on a rectilinear lot.

Sometimes angling a deck off the back of a house can have a dramatic effect. Besides leading people to a certain part of the yard, it can open up the area alongside the deck for other purposes, such as play space or permanent landscaping.

Tie in overhead. Incorporating an arbor or overhang into your deck design can do much more than provide shade. An overhead connects the vertical mass of the house to the horizontal expanse of the deck. It also yields a look of partial enclosure, which adds to your sense of privacy when you are outdoors.

Vary decking direction. The lines created by decking tend to direct the eye. Consequently, the direction in which you lay the deck boards can have a surprising impact on how people view the deck and the rest of your property. For instance, setting decking parallel to the back of the house makes the deck seem narrower.

By angling deck boards you can direct attention to a spectacular view or beautiful part of your garden. You can also change the direction of the decking to create patterns, making the deck more visually interesting and adding an illusion of depth. If overdone, though, this device can make a deck's surface pattern seem too busy or contrived.

Choose detailing thoughtfully. A little extra attention paid to the details of a deck can add greatly to its style and substance. Improve the workmanship of the railing and benches, and the whole deck looks more intensively crafted. Add fascia boards around the edges of the decking, and the entire structure becomes more cleanly defined. Build a skirt around the outside of the deck to cover the substructure, and you add a sense of mass and permanence.

DECK MATERIALS

The materials from which you build your deck affect its ease of construction, strength, longevity, and appearance. How accurately you estimate what quantities of these materials you need will save you money and time.

Lumber Selection

Lumber is usually the most expensive component of a deck. Becoming familiar with types of wood and lumberyard terminology can not only save you money, but help you avoid costly mistakes that might shorten the life of your deck.

Lumber is categorized as hardwood or softwood, designations that have little to do with its relative strength. Hardwoods simply come from deciduous or broad-leafed trees, such as oaks and maples. Softwoods come from conifers, such as redwoods and cedar. Because softwoods are generally cheaper and easier to work with, most decks are constructed from them.

Lumber is further categorized by the species of tree it comes from and by which part of the tree it is cut from. Any part of a deck that will be within 6 inches of soil or embedded in concrete should be built from Heart redwood, cedar, or cypress. They are the most decay-resistant woods (you can also use treated lumber). Heartwood is taken from the center of the tree and is darker in color than sapwood, which comes from closer to the bark. Because it is also richer in texture, heartwood is often preferred for deck surfaces and other exposed features.

Besides appearance and decay resistance, the tree species also affects a wood's strength, tendency to warp, and workability. The guide to commonly used softwoods printed inside the front cover of this book will help you choose the right wood for the job you need done. For instance, you may want Heart redwood for deck boards, but prefer a less expensive but equally strong wood, like Douglas fir, for the deck's substructure.

Regional availability determines which lumber is the best buy. You can find out what's available at your local lumberyard. A salesperson can acquaint you with grades of lumber, which are based on the wood's grain, moisture content, and relative number of defects such as knots; each of these attributes affects both price and appearance.

Individually selecting each piece of lumber you'll use for your deck is time well spent, particularly if you use a less expensive grade. This way, you can reject boards with cracks or splits and ones that are warped or cupped.

You will also find that lumber is sold "rough" or "surfaced." Surfaced lumber, which is required for decking, is sold by its nominal size before being surfaced and dried. Consequently, a board sold as a 2 by 4 actually measures 1½ inches by 3½ inches.

Treated Lumber

Using treated lumber for posts and other supports that come close to or in contact with soil or are embedded in concrete may save you money and also increase the life of your deck. However, using this lumber, which is usually green- or brown-tinted, has drawbacks. Besides being an unnatural color, treated lumber is more brittle and harder to nail than redwood or cedar. It also warps more easily. Finally, the Environmental Protection Agency has issued precautions about chemically treated wood: wear goggles and breathing protection when cutting treated lumber, and never burn it.

TYPICAL DECK FASTENERS

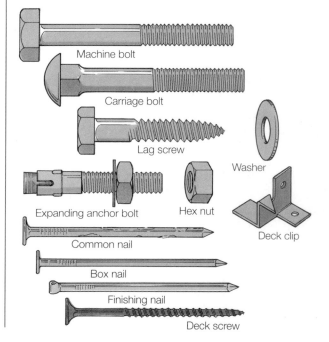

Machine bolt

Carriage bolt

Lag screw

Washer

Expanding anchor bolt

Hex nut

Deck clip

Common nail

Box nail

Finishing nail

Deck screw

FRAMING CONNECTORS

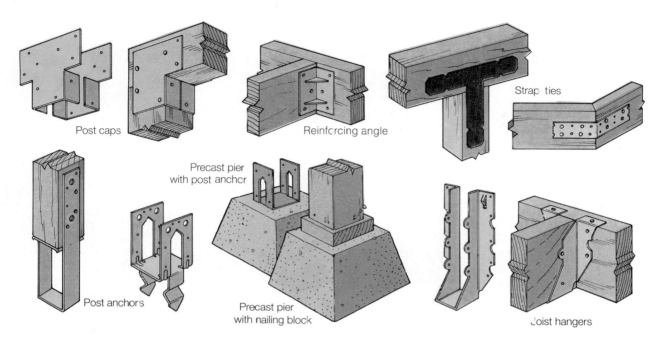

Post caps

Reinforcing angle

Strap ties

Precast pier with post anchor

Post anchors

Precast pier with nailing block

Joist hangers

Hardware

Hot-dipped galvanized common or box nails are used for most outdoor deck construction. If you want particularly secure decking, use galvanized deck screws to attach deck boards to joists. Drive these with a power screwdriver or use an electric drill with a screwdriver tip.

If you'd like a particularly clean-looking deck surface, use deck clips. Nailed to the side of decking lumber and secured to the joists, these relatively expensive connectors eliminate visible nail heads.

In main structural connections, use bolts or lag screws. To accommodate the necessary washers and nuts, bolts should be about an inch longer than the combined thickness of the pieces to be bolted together. When using lag screws, drill pilot holes about two-thirds the length of the lag screws, using a drill ⅛ inch smaller in diameter than the lag screw's shank.

To join a ledger to a masonry wall, use expanding anchor bolts.

The illustration above shows the most commonly available framing connectors, including joist hangers, post anchors, post caps, and framing anchors. Metal connectors can help prevent lumber splits commonly caused by toenailing two boards together. They are easy to use and they strengthen the connections.

Piers & Footings

There are a number of ways to anchor a deck to the ground. The easiest is to pour concrete footings, then set precast piers, available in hardware stores, on the surface. Precast piers come with nailing boards on top or with embedded anchors for attaching posts (see illustration above). Or, you can form your own concrete piers with wooden forms and embed post anchors in the tops.

For deeper footings, buy tubular concrete forms, cut them to the needed length, place into holes, and fill with concrete. Embed post anchors at tops. Wet-cure all poured concrete one week. Then remove forms.

Preservatives & Sealers

There is no substitute for using decay-resistant wood like Heart redwood or pressure-treated lumber where deck members come in contact with soil or are embedded in concrete. Using any other wood or trying to apply preservatives yourself cannot be as satisfactory. Doing so will only decrease the life and stability of your deck.

Applying a water repellent, stain (even pastel-tinted), or paint and doing some strategic caulking can, however, protect other parts of a deck and preserve its beauty. Product labels tell you how many coats to apply.

READING PLANS

Learning to interpret the different types of architectural drawing shown in this book will help you visualize how the deck will relate to your house and garden and make building it much easier. It will also simplify the process of planning any modifications in construction.

Plan view

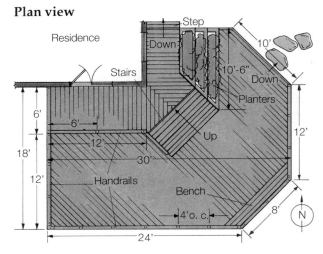

A plan view shows the deck from above. It gives the scale of the deck in relation to the house and indicates the decking pattern. Since it includes horizontal measurements, a plan view also allows you to visualize circulation and judge the sizes of different areas.

Plan view of framing & foundation

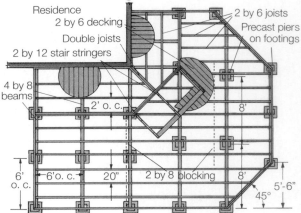

A framing plan also shows the deck from above, except that decking is removed to show the substructure—sizes, quantities, and distances between joists, beams, and posts ("o. c." stands for "on center"—center-to-center measurement). This view is useful for ordering materials.

Elevation section

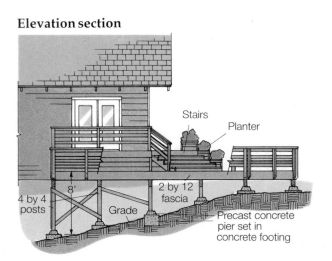

An elevation is a side view of the deck. An elevation section is a side view of a slice somewhere in the deck, often located by letters on the plan views. Elevations reveal vertical dimensions and relationships.

Railing detail

A detail drawing gives you a close-up of a particular feature of the deck, such as a bench, railing, or stair, whose construction is not apparent in a plan view or elevation section.

DECK ANATOMY

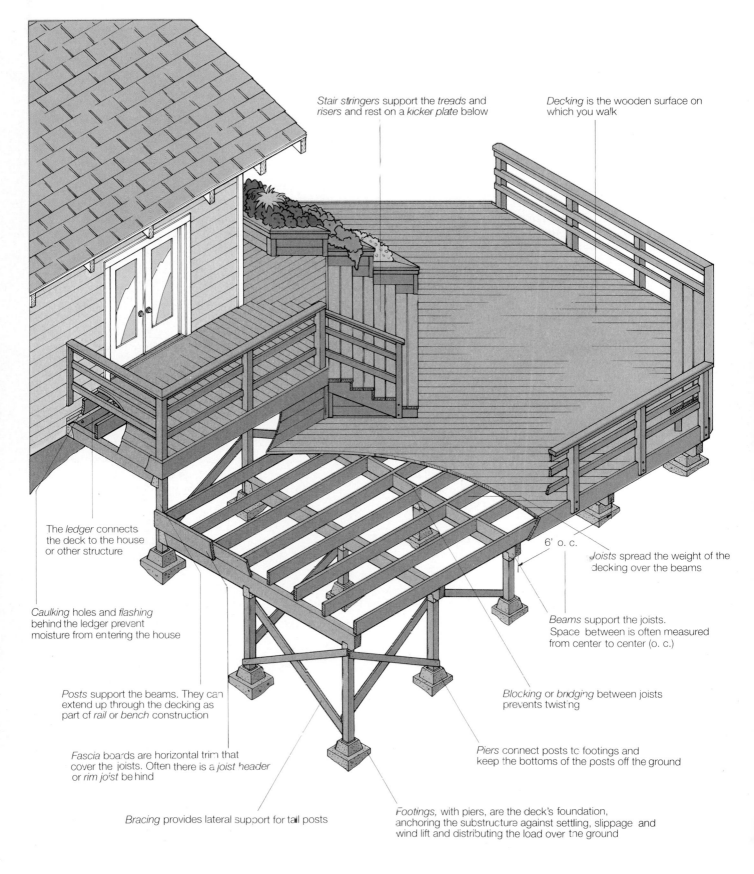

Stair stringers support the treads and risers and rest on a kicker plate below

Decking is the wooden surface on which you walk

The ledger connects the deck to the house or other structure

Caulking holes and flashing behind the ledger prevent moisture from entering the house

Posts support the beams. They can extend up through the decking as part of rail or bench construction

Fascia boards are horizontal trim that cover the joists. Often there is a joist header or rim joist behind

Bracing provides lateral support for tall posts

6' o. c.

Joists spread the weight of the decking over the beams

Beams support the joists. Space between is often measured from center to center (o. c.)

Blocking or bridging between joists prevents twisting

Piers connect posts to footings and keep the bottoms of the posts off the ground

Footings, with piers, are the deck's foundation, anchoring the substructure against settling, slippage and wind lift and distributing the load over the ground

ADJUSTING PLANS

Chances are good that none of the plans in this book will fit your needs exactly. The dimensions of your property will probably call for a slightly larger, smaller, wider, or narrower deck, so you'll probably need to make adjustments in the design you choose. You might also want to adjust plans to make the deck better complement your house and the natural terrain of your lot, or suit your style of outdoor living. How easily you can do this will depend on your understanding of deck construction.

To make adjustments, think about a deck from the top down. In other words, draw exactly what you want the deck to look like from a bird's-eye view (see page 16), then make the appropriate changes in the substructure, working from the joists to the beams to the posts to the footings.

Our charts of maximum loads and spans will be very important to making any changes. Sometimes, you can change the size or configuration of the deck simply by increasing the length of certain deck members, such as beams and joists. At other times, increasing the length of one member will make it absolutely necessary to increase its size or add additional supports. For example, if you increase the length of a beam to handle additional joists, you may also need to increase its size or add more posts to support it properly.

To Raise or Lower a Deck

Raising the height of the deck often means more than simply using taller posts. If you raise it more than 30 inches above the ground, you should also add railings for safety (required by most codes). If you go higher than 5 feet, you'll need to cross-brace the posts.

If you lower a deck, make sure there is at least 8 inches between the ground and wooden deck members. This clearance may require some excavation. Wood set that close to the ground should be pressure-treated; or use decay-resistant heartwood.

To Make a Deck Larger

This is usually fairly easy. Depending on the deck's configuration, simply increase the length (you may have to do some splicing if you are making big changes) or number of joists and beams. If necessary, add posts and piers to support the new beams. If you are increasing the size of the deck along the side that adjoins the house, you'll also have to increase the length of the ledger.

You can safely extend joists over the outside beam to enlarge a deck as long as you don't exceed half the joist span between the ledger and beam.

WHEN YOUR DECK CHANGES HEIGHTS & LEVELS

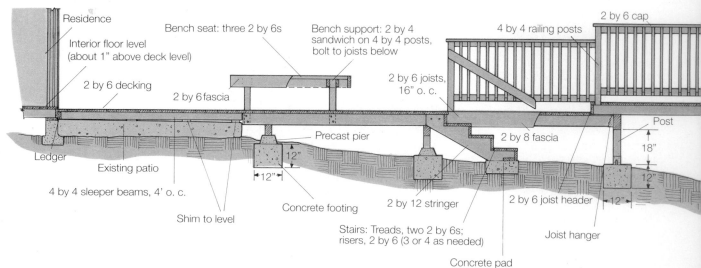

Residence
Interior floor level (about 1" above deck level)
2 by 6 decking
Ledger
Existing patio
4 by 4 sleeper beams, 4' o. c.
Shim to level
2 by 6 fascia
Bench seat: three 2 by 6s
Bench support: 2 by 4 sandwich on 4 by 4 posts, bolt to joists below
Precast pier
12"
12"
Concrete footing
Stairs: Treads, two 2 by 6s; risers, 2 by 6 (3 or 4 as needed)
2 by 12 stringer
Concrete pad with kicker plate
2 by 6 joists, 16" o. c.
4 by 4 railing posts
2 by 6 cap
2 by 8 fascia
Post
18"
2 by 6 joist header
12"
Joist hanger

To Make a Deck Smaller

This is just the opposite of enlarging a deck. Shorten or decrease the number of joists and beams and, if necessary, shorten the ledger or decrease the distance between ledger and beam. Then reposition posts and footings accordingly.

To Make a Deck Multilevel

One of the easiest ways to change a single-level deck into a multilevel one is to vary post height between deck levels. Attach a stringer along the posts at the higher level and use it like a ledger to support the lower deck's joists. Of course, you'll also have to add steps if the difference between deck levels is more than 8 inches.

If you prefer that the distance between levels be only one step, you can accomplish this by constructing the upper level with joists resting on top of beams, then using joist hangers for the lower level. This way, the lower joists are at the same level as the tops of the beams and the width of the joists below the upper level.

If the upper deck will be very small, create multiple levels by building the framing of the deck as though it were for one level, then adding a second layer of joists (at right angles) on top of the first.

Whenever you build a multilevel deck, alternate decking directions between levels. Usually the framing will require this anyway, but the end result is a safer separation between levels.

Plan view of framing: Adjusted deck plan

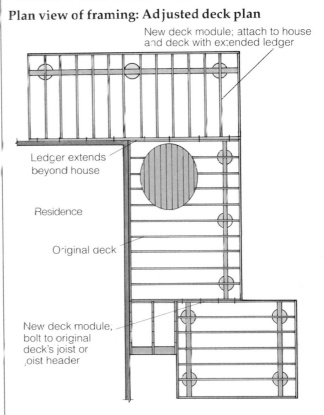

New deck module; attach to house and deck with extended ledger

Ledger extends beyond house

Residence

Original deck

New deck module; bolt to original deck's joist or joist header

To Change a Deck's Shape

This is simplest with square or rectangular decks. Basically, you follow the same rules as for enlarging or decreasing a deck's size, adjusting the length and number of appropriate joists and beams, increasing their size as necessary, and designing an adequate substructure.

You can build a larger deck by linking together smaller, simpler modules. For example, begin by following one of the plans in the book to build a module or section that attaches to the house. Then attach other sections to this basic module, using common beams. You can also connect decks at an outside joist so long as you increase the size of the joist so it is as strong as a beam.

One way to wrap a deck around your house is to extend the ledger out past the corner so that it acts as a beam for the secondary side of the deck. You might have to increase the ledger's size or double up the extended portion to enable it to handle the load. Then add new beams and joists according to your decking pattern for the secondary side. See the illustration above.

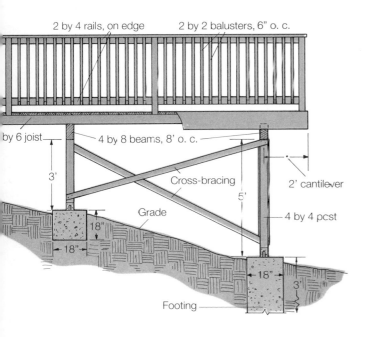

2 by 4 rails, on edge   2 by 2 balusters, 6" o. c.

by 6 joist

4 by 8 beams, 8' o. c.

3'

Cross-bracing

2' cantilever

5'

Grade

4 by 4 post

18"

18"

18"

3'

Footing

CHARTING THE SPANS

Use the five tables here to figure the proper sizes, spans, and heights for your deck's structural elements. The figures given in the tables are recommended maximums; you can always choose shorter spans, closer spacings, or larger lumber. Different designers will often recommend different figures. Consult your local building department to be sure you're meeting all local codes.

Although you'll build your deck from the footings up, it's often simplest to begin planning from the top down, working back and forth until you find the best joist-beam-post combination. Some design solutions may be more desirable since they require less lumber, easier-to-handle beams, less space, or fewer footings.

Table 1: Softwood Strength Groupings. Use this table to learn the strength grouping of the wood species you plan to use in your deck. You may find it more economical to use different woods for different parts; for example, you may opt for redwood decking with a pressure-treated fir substructure.

Table 2: Decking Spans. Now select the size of decking boards. Then, using the Table 1 strength group, calculate the maximum distance your decking should span between joists—or between beams, if your design calls for sleeper construction. (Sleepers are beams laid directly onto a firm, solid surface.)

Table 3: Joist Sizes & Spans. Next, use the information you've gathered from tables 1 and 2 to determine the correct size and beam-to-beam span of joists for the spacings determined in Table 2. You can start with either your joist size or your joist span—the chart will provide the other one.

Table 4: Beam Sizes & Spans. Again, use the strength groupings (Table 1) to determine which size beams will span from post to post when set various distances apart. (You may be limited by the beam sizes available.) For this table, you may round down to the nearest whole foot.

Table 5: Minimum Post Sizes. To determine post size, you need to know the wood grouping (Table 1), the joist span or beam-to-beam spacing (Table 3), and the beam span or post-to-post spacing (Table 4). Multiply the beam spacing (in feet) by the post spacing (in feet) to determine the load area (in square feet) that each post supports. Then, from Table 5, select a post size that meets your height requirements. In order to simplify construction, try to use posts and beams of the same thickness.

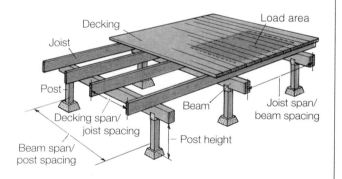

Table 1: Softwood Strength Groupings

(Based on No. 2 & Better)

Group A	Douglas fir, Western hemlock, Western larch, Southern pine, coast Sitka spruce
Group B	Western cedar, Douglas fir (South), hem-fir, Alpine white fir, Eastern mountain hemlock, pine (all but Southern), redwood (Clear only), spruce (Eastern, Engelmann, Sitka)
Group C	Northern white cedar, redwood (Construction Heart & Better)

Table 2: Decking Sizes & Spans

Maximum suggested decking spans, or joist spacings, are shown. Greater spans are allowable with some decking material, but may result in an overly springy deck. Spans assume normal loads, distributed evenly.

	Species Group (see Table 1)		
	A	B	C
Nominal 1-inch boards laid flat	16″	14″	12″
Nominal 2-inch lumber laid flat	24″	24″	24″
2 by 3s laid on edge	48″	36″	32″
2 by 4s laid on edge	60″	60″	60″

Table 3: Joist Sizes & Spans

Joist spans, or beam spacings, are measured from center to center of beams or supports based on No. 2 & Better joists placed on edge. Maximums are given.

	Maximum Span per Species Group (see Table 1)		
	A	**B**	**C**
16″ joist spacings:			
2 by 6	9′9″	8′7″	7′9″
2 by 8	12′10″	11′4″	10′2″
2 by 10	16′5″	14′6″	13′
24″ joist spacings:			
2 by 6	8′6″	7′6″	6′9″
2 by 8	11′3″	9′11″	8′11″
2 by 10	14′4″	12′8″	11′4″
32″ joist spacings:			
2 by 6	7′9″	6′10″	6′2″
2 by 8	10′2″	9′	8′1″
2 by 10	13′	11′6″	10′4″

Table 5: Minimum Post Sizes

Proper post size depends on overall load area and post height. To figure load area, multiply beam spacing (joist span) by post spacing (beam span). Round up to next largest load area listed below. Sizes are based on Standard & Better for 4 by 4 posts, No. 1 & Better for larger sizes.

Species Group (see Table 1)	Post Size (nominal)	36	48	60	72	84	96	108	120	132	144
A	4 by 4	Up to 12′ high				Up to 10′ high			Up to 8′ high		
	4 by 6					Up to 12′ →				Up to 10′	
	6 by 6								Up to 12′		
B	4 by 4	Up to 12′		Up to 10′ →		Up to 8′ →					
	4 by 6			Up to 12′ →			Up to 10′ →				
	6 by 6					Up to 12′ →					
C	4 by 4	Up to 12′	Up to 10′		Up to 8′ →		Up to 6′ →				
	4 by 6		Up to 12′		Up to 10′ →		Up to 8′ →				
	6 by 6			Up to 12′ →							

Table 4: Beam Sizes & Spans

Beam spans, or post spacings, are from center to center of posts or supports based on No. 2 & Better beams placed on edge.

Figures refer to dimensioned (not built-up or laminated) lumber only. Round down to the nearest whole foot.

Species Group (see Table 1)	Beam Size (nominal)	4′	5′	6′	7′	8′	9′	10′	11′	12′
A	4 by 6	Up to 6′ spans →								
	3 by 8	Up to 8′ →		Up to 7′	Up to 6′ →					
	4 by 8	Up to 10′	Up to 9′	Up to 8′	Up to 7′ →		Up to 6′ →			
	3 by 10	Up to 11′	Up to 10′	Up to 9′	Up to 8′ →		Up to 7′ →		Up to 6′ →	
	4 by 10	Up to 12′	Up to 11′	Up to 10′	Up to 9′	Up to 8′ →		Up to 7′ →		
	3 by 12		Up to 12′	Up to 11′	Up to 10′	Up to 9′ →		Up to 8′ →		
	4 by 12			Up to 12′ →		Up to 11′	Up to 10′ →		Up to 9′ →	
	6 by 10					Up to 12′	Up to 11′	Up to 10′ →		
B	4 by 6	Up to 6′ →								
	3 by 8	Up to 7′ →		Up to 6′ →						
	4 by 8	Up to 9′	Up to 8′	Up to 7′ →		Up to 6′ →				
	3 by 10	Up to 10′	Up to 9′	Up to 8′	Up to 7′ →		Up to 6′ →			
	4 by 10	Up to 11′	Up to 10′	Up to 9′	Up to 8′ →		Up to 7′ →			Up to 6′
	3 by 12	Up to 12′	Up to 11′	Up to 10′	Up to 9′	Up to 8′ →		Up to 7′ →		
	4 by 12		Up to 12′	Up to 11′	Up to 10′	Up to 9′ →		Up to 8′ →		
	6 by 10			Up to 12′	Up to 11′	Up to 10′	Up to 9′ →			
C	4 by 6	Up to 6′								
	3 by 8	Up to 7′	Up to 6′							
	4 by 8	Up to 8′	Up to 7′	Up to 6′ →						
	3 by 10	Up to 9′	Up to 8′	Up to 7′	Up to 6′ →					
	4 by 10	Up to 10′	Up to 9′	Up to 8′ →		Up to 7′ →		Up to 6′ →		
	3 by 12	Up to 11′	Up to 10′	Up to 9′	Up to 8′	Up to 7′ →			Up to 6′ →	
	4 by 12	Up to 12′	Up to 11′	Up to 10′	Up to 9′ →		Up to 8′ →		Up to 7′ →	
	6 by 10		Up to 12′	Up to 11′	Up to 10′	Up to 9′ →		Up to 8′ →		

BUILDING YOUR DECK

When building your new deck, you should follow the construction sequence shown below and on the opposite page. For homeowners who lack construction experience or want to modify plans, Sunset's *Decks* book can supplement this outline with more extensive instruction. It expands on each of these basic steps and also discusses alternative methods of construction.

Before beginning work, have all plans, permits, materials, and tools on hand (see page 26 and inside of back cover). Start by preparing the site; kill and remove all weeds, remove large rocks and debris. Ensure adequate drainage either by sloping the grade away from the house and deck or by installing drainpipes; pooled water below the deck will attract insects and small animals.

1. Attach ledger. *Anchor the deck by attaching a ledger to an outside house wall so that top of deck will be 1 inch below interior floor level. Lag-screw into wood siding, anchor bolt into masonry. Flash; if needed, caulk to prevent water damage.*

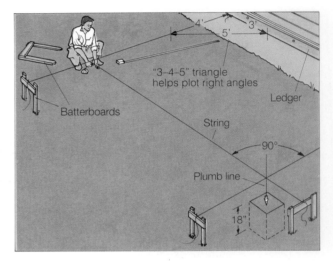

2. Locate footings. *Use a measuring tape, taut string, and batterboards to outline the deck, making sure corners are square or properly angled. Use a plumb bob to locate corner footings first. Stretch additional strings to locate interior footings.*

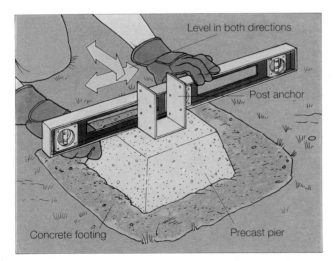

3. Set footings and piers. *Dig holes as specified by local codes. Fill with concrete, and while it sets, soak precast piers in water. When firm enough, set piers into these footings. Level everything. Cure several days.*

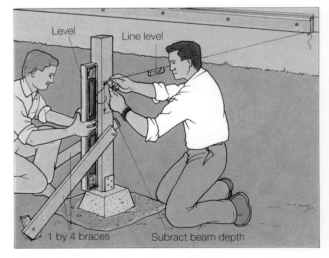

4. Attach posts to piers. *Place and plumb each post. Stretch level string or 2 by 4 from where joist bottoms will meet the ledger to each post. Mark the post, subtract the depth of the beam, then cut. Attach post to pier; brace temporarily.*

Toolbox Checklist

Brushes, rollers (to apply finish)
Carpenter's level
Chalkline
Chalk or pencil
Chisel
Combination square
Crescent wrench
Extension cord
Framing square

Hammer
Handsaw
Hoe (to mix concrete)
Hose (to mix concrete)
Line level
Nailset
Plumb bob
Portable circular saw
Portable drill

Screwdrivers
Shims or spacers
Shovel
Socket wrench
Stakes or batterboards
String
Tape measure (50–100 feet)
Wheelbarrow (to mix concrete)
Work gloves

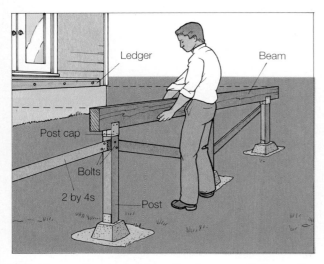

5. Set beams. *For sleepers, toenail or lag-screw the beams directly to pier nailing blocks. For those on posts, raise beams to post tops and attach with post cap connectors. For decks over 3 feet high, attach cross-bracing between posts.*

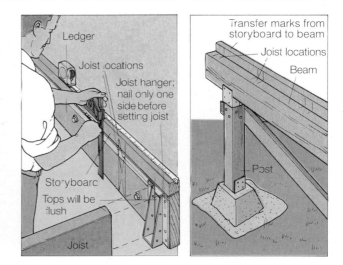

6. Install joists. *Start at an outside corner and use a storyboard, tape measure, and combination square to mark joist locations on ledger or first beam. Transfer measurements from storyboard to opposite beam. Attach joists (crown side up).*

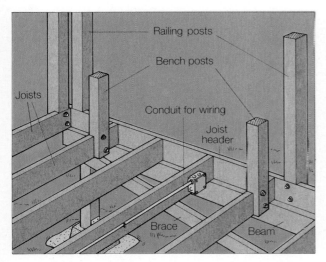

7. Finish stairs, railings, and benches. *Amenities with supports tied to the deck's substructure should be completed now. Install electrical wiring, plumbing, or drip irrigation needs and black plastic to prevent weeds.*

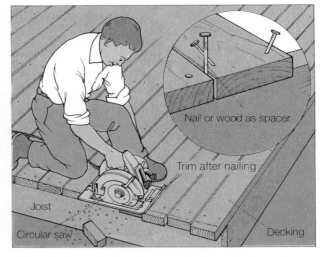

8. Lay decking. *Lay boards, cup-side down, starting at one end of the deck. Use a large nail or piece of wood (about ¼" thick) as a consistent spacer between boards. Nail at opposing angles, mark board ends, then trim with a circular saw.*

DECKS IN DETAIL

Using one of the 15 professionally designed deck plans in this chapter will enhance your home's individuality, generate a more professional-looking project, and increase the value of your property. Differences in plan styles, foundations, materials, and details reflect the individual designers' preferences. All of the decks in this chapter have been built successfully. You will be able to build them, too, if you're moderately skilled and have a helper. Or you may choose to have a plan built by a contractor. Either way, one of these designs will be right for you.

No two sites are alike; no two households have the same needs. The plans are shown as designed for specific sites; you'll want to adjust them to your own needs. Variations may be influenced by locale, style, needs, and cost. Scale your deck in relation to your house: too large a deck wastes space and wood; too small a deck can look skimpy. Angles, elevation changes, and curves add interest to large decks and create an illusion of space on small ones. Landscaping will blend the deck with your garden.

Read all the plans for useful design and building tips. Before you begin, check with building authorities regarding soil conditions, local codes, and required permits. Remember, building is full of surprises! Expect to make minor changes as you go along.

Cantilevered over a slope, this sleek redwood deck provides extra entertaining space. Natural features can be enjoyed from built-in benches. See page 27 for plans.

Each plan in this chapter includes a materials list. However, since houses and the people who live in them vary, you'll want to adapt those plans.

Inside the back cover of this book is a blank materials list that, along with these tips and advice from your local supplier, will help you to more accurately order what you need to build your deck.

These basic rules will help you cut the cost of materials:

- Get bids from several suppliers.
- Order as many materials as possible at one time and place.
- Order readily available materials in standard dimensions.
- Allow an extra five to ten percent for waste and blemished goods.
- Know your suppliers' return policies.

Lumber. The best way to order lumber for the substructure of your deck is to make a list from the final plan.

To estimate decking, laid ³/₁₆" apart, use one of these formulas:

- Number of 2 by 4s laid flat = 3.3 x width of deck (in feet).
- Number of 2 by 6s laid flat = 2.1 x width of deck (in feet).
- Number of 2 by 2s (or edge-laid 2 by 3s or 2 by 4s) = 7.1 x width of deck (in feet).

Round results up to the next highest foot. That will give you the number of single boards needed to span the width of the deck. Then, if

necessary, you can order the appropriate number of shorter pieces to cover each span. In other words, if the above calculation says you need 100 16-foot 2 by 4s, you'll probably want 200 8-footers instead.

Concrete and masonry. You'll probably need a pier or footing for every post. Casting your own piers is an option; buying precast piers is easier. You'll also need footings for stairs. Use the dimensions of your footings to calculate the total cubic volume of concrete you'll need: 1 foot x 1 foot x 1 foot = 1 cubic foot; 27 cubic feet = 1 cubic yard. One 90-pound bag of premixed concrete will fill ⅔ cubic foot.

Order ready-to-use concrete, (delivered) by the cubic yard.

A bed of gravel, 3 to 6 inches deep, provides good drainage under footings.

Hardware. Nails are sold by weight. Use hot-dipped galvanized common or box nails for construction; finish nails for trim.

Many of the deck plans specify nail size. If not, use a nail that is about 2½ times as long as the thickness of the top board you are nailing.

When laying decking, secure decking boards to joists with two nails at each place where they join. To calculate the number of nails needed, begin with the number of decking boards you will be using (see above), then multiply that figure by the number of joists they will cross. Double the answer. See the chart (below left) to convert number of nails to pounds. Increase the amount to accommodate other members you'll be nailing. Since nails are relatively inexpensive, and you can always use leftovers, it's best to order extras.

To estimate other hardware, go to the plan and start counting. Wood screws should be long enough so that the thread is completely embedded in the bottom board. To accommodate

washers and nuts, buy bolts 1 inch longer than the combined thickness of the pieces you're connecting. (For amounts, see below.)

When ordering connectors, such as joist hangers, make sure you also order nails to go with them.

Ready-made aluminum or galvanized sheet metal Z-flashing for the ledger is sold in 10-foot sections. Order caulking to pack fastener holes and to seal other gaps created when attaching the ledger.

Finishes. Labels will tell you how many square feet the product will cover. Read the instructions to learn how many coats of a paint, stain, or sealer to apply.

Other materials. Additional needs may include waterproof membranes for roof decks and metal inserts for planters. In most cases, if you have the exact dimensions of the deck or amenity, your local building supply store will help you order or locate the right materials.

How Many Nails per Pound

	Common	Box	Finish
8d (2½")	106	145	189
9d (2¾")	96	132	172
10d (3")	69	121	132
12d (3¼")	64	94	113
16d (3½")	49	71	90

Bolt & Lag Screw Locations

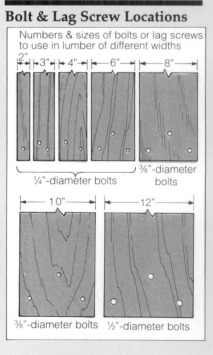

Numbers & sizes of bolts or lag screws to use in lumber of different widths

2" 3" 4" 6" 8"

¼"-diameter bolts
⅜"-diameter bolts

10" 12"

⅜"-diameter bolts ½"-diameter bolts

ELEGANT EXTENSION

Cantilevered over a slope and around an olive tree and a boulder, this deck works with a brick patio to provide pleasantly varied outdoor living space.

Design: Gary McCook, Landscape Contractor

MATERIALS LIST*

Use pressure-treated Douglas fir for structural members, surfaced redwood for visible members, and galvanized hardware.

Lumber

Posts	4 by 4
Beams	4 by 12; 4 by 10 on 16" footings
Joists/Blocking	2 by 10
Ledgers	2 by 10
Bracing	2 by 6
Decking	2 by 6
Fascia	2 by 8; 1 by 4
Open Railings	4 by 4 posts; 2 by 6 cap; 2 by 4 rail; 2 by 2 balusters
Fence/Railing	2 by 8 cap; 2 by 4 framing; 1 by 12 siding; 1 by 4 batters
Bench	2 by 6 backs, seats, front plate; 2 by 4 supports, back plate

Other	2 by 8 plate on grade beam

Masonry

Cement	8" by 24"-deep (continuous) grade beam; 24" by 32"-deep footings; 16" by 24"-deep footings

Hardware

Nails	16d
Bolts	$5/16$" by 5" machine bolts at rail balusters-to-header; ½" by 10" anchor bolts at plate-to-grade beam ½" by 7" machine bolts at rail posts-to-header
Connectors	Joist hangers at ledger; 12" T straps at post-to-beam; 2$1/16$" by 2$3^5/16$" strap ties at beam-to-beam; post anchors; post caps; nails or screws as required for each
Other	#5 reinforcing bars in concrete; low-voltage light fixtures

*To determine the amount of materials needed for your deck, consult the guide on page 26.

This long, low deck chooses to integrate natural features of the site rather than resist them. The downslope, spreading tree, and substantial boulder are all accepted parts of an aesthetically satisfying design (see photo on page 24).

Cantilevering over a slope extends the view. And running the diagonal decking parallel to the long side of the plan emphasizes the new expansiveness of the outdoor area.

To Adapt This Plan

You may want to modify the height of the deck, depending on your slope, and the design of the fence/railing behind the bench. The shape of the deck will be influenced by the shape of the side of your house and by the locations of any natural features you incorporate. But the exterior lines and subtle level changes can work successfully in a wide variety of situations.

The railing might be opened to a staircase going downhill or to a broad step to garden level.

Although designed as a cantilevered platform, this deck, with its clean low profile, is suitable at lesser heights or even in a flat yard where, with its closed fence and generous bench (and storage potential), it could serve well as a children's play area.

The board-and-batten railing is designed to match the side of the house. You can easily adapt this to your own siding, whether it is shingled or covered in lapped or tongue-and-groove boards. (Near a masonry house, select a compatible material such as beveled siding to echo the lines of window shutters or use a basketweave trellis to repeat the pattern of brick walls.) First build a securely attached frame of posts and rails; then cover with the desired decorative element.

Decking

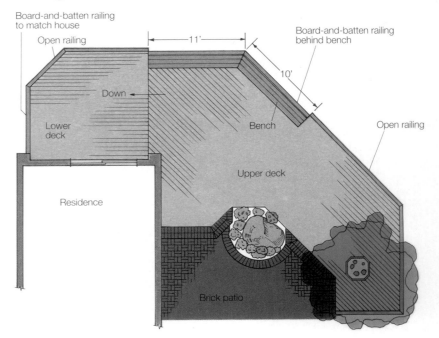

Grade beam detail

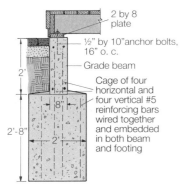

Footing detail

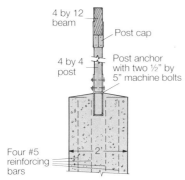

Building Notes

Before building a cantilevered deck, check with an architect or structural engineer to be sure the foundation plan is correct in relation to your particular site (also see span charts on pages 20–21).

To properly connect the two beams that meet at the 135° angle, miter their ends so they butt together, centered over the post. At both inner and outer sides of the joint, bend a 12" by 12" T strap to fit across both beam-to-beam and beam-to-post

Plan view of framing & foundation

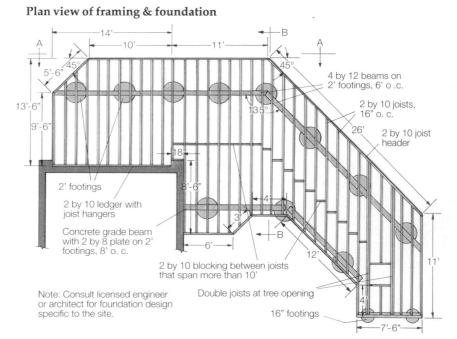

seams; then attach. Leave room above it to attach an additional 2¹⁄₁₆" by 23⁵⁄₁₆" strap tie. Be certain this meets your local code; otherwise you may have to have two steel connectors custom-fabricated.

Attach the railing's 4 by 4 posts and 2 by 2 balusters with ⁵⁄₁₆" by 5" machine bolts that extend through the post or baluster, the fascia, and the header behind. This will provide greater strength than first attaching the fascia to the header and then attaching the railing to the fascia.

When building the benches, consider using the space beneath the seat for storage. You could provide access doors at the ends or build a portion of the seat on a hinged frame to be lifted for access. Waterproof the insides.

Elevation section A

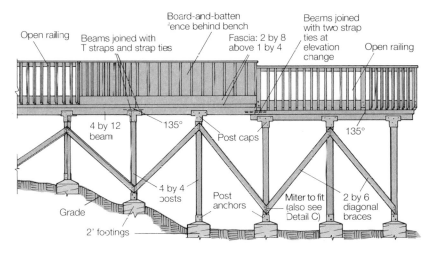

Elevation section B

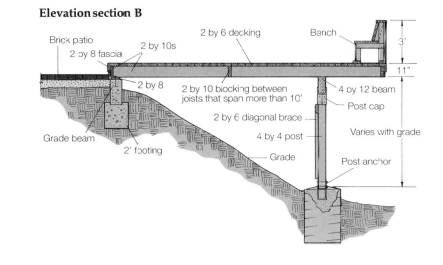

Detail C: Plan view of alternate brace attachment

Open railing detail

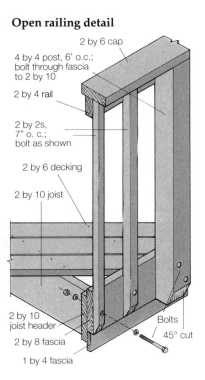

Board-and-batten detail

Bench detail

SUM OF THE PARTS

"I retained the existing gazebo and added a lawn, patio, and decking to complement it. Together, they surround the new fish pond, create a focal interest, and suggest oriental balance and style."

Design: Jolee Horne, Landscape Designer

Tying pre-existing areas together, this design is organized around a central fish pond—an element that gives the whole setting a sense of tranquility (see photo on page 2). As a result, the rectangular decks, gazebo (one step up) and distant patio all become more functional. Decking is all on a single, low level, but the change in surface board size and direction adds interest to the quiet and serene design. Simple geometric shapes contribute to the ordered feeling.

To Adapt This Plan

A small, level yard containing separate, presently unconnected elements is a perfect place to build this deck. If you have an unused area, perhaps behind your garage or in a large side yard, this plan could yield a secluded retreat. It could also be used to impart organization to a large, flat yard.

Think of each deck as a separate unit; this plan has four, but you could drop or add a component. You can change the length or width of any unit to link existing elements in your garden. Be sure to place the focal point where it will divert the eye from any unsightly or distracting view.

Building Notes

The 4 by 4 beams are nailed directly to the precast pier blocks. However, a low-level deck plan like this one could be set directly onto an existing slab. Then, the beams would be called sleepers.

To prevent weeds and simplify future garden maintenance, begin by using a pre-emergent weed killer, then lay 4- to 6-mil polyethylene sheeting covered with gravel where the decks will be built.

MATERIALS LIST*

Use pressure-treated lumber for structural members, surfaced redwood (grade is specified) for visible members, and galvanized hardware.

FOR DECKS

Lumber

Beams	4 by 4
Decking	Clear All Heart
	2 by 4 for small decks
	2 by 6 for large deck
Fascia	2 by 4 Select

Masonry

Piers	Precast concrete
Concrete	12" by 12" by 12" footings

Hardware

Nails	16d or 12d, or wood screws

FOR BENCHES

Lumber

Posts	4 by 4 Construction Heart
Bracing	2 by 6 Clear All Heart
Seating	2 by 6 Clear
Fascia	2 by 4 Clear

Masonry

Cement	12" by 12' by 18" footings
Gravel	4"- to 6"-deep drain rock

Hardware

Nails	16d or 12d
Bolts	½" by 8½" carriage bolts with washers and nuts

*To determine the amount of materials needed for your deck, consult the guide on page 26.

Plan view of decking & benches

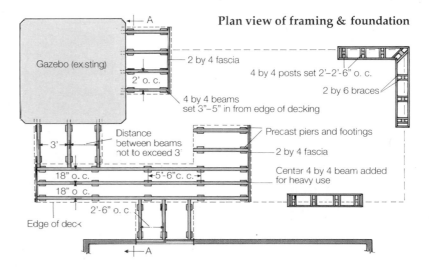

- 11'
- 4'-1"
- A
- 4 by 4
- Staggered nailing pattern
- Decking
- Corner bench
- 7'-5"
- 11'
- 23'-3"
- Gazebo (existing)
- 7'
- Lawn
- 6'
- 8'-5'
- 7'
- 4'-1"
- 3'
- 5'-11"
- Fish pond
- 16¾"
- 4'-4"
- 9'-6"
- Patio
- 8'-2½"
- 3'-10'
- Bench
- 16¾"
- 7'
- 10'-6"
- 7'-8"
- 6'
- 22'-5'
- Residence
- A

Plan view of framing & foundation

- A
- Gazebo (existing)
- 2 by 4 fascia
- 4 by 4 posts set 2'–2'-6" o. c.
- 2' o. c.
- 2 by 6 braces
- 4 by 4 beams set 3"–5" in from edge of decking
- Precast piers and footings
- Distance between beams not to exceed 3'
- 2 by 4 fascia
- 3'
- Center 4 by 4 beam added for heavy use
- 18" o. c.
- 5'-6" c. c.
- 18" o. c.
- 2'-6" o. c.
- Edge of deck
- A

Bench detail

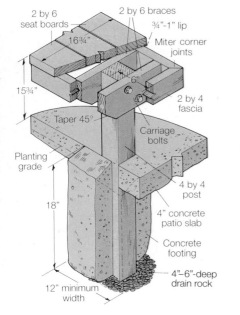

- 2 by 6 seat boards
- 2 by 6 braces
- ¾"–1" lip
- 16¾"
- Miter corner joints
- 15¾"
- 6"
- 2 by 4 fascia
- Taper 45°
- Carriage bolts
- Planting grade
- 4 by 4 post
- 4" concrete patio slab
- 18"
- Concrete footing
- 4"–6"-deep drain rock
- 12" minimum width

Elevation section A

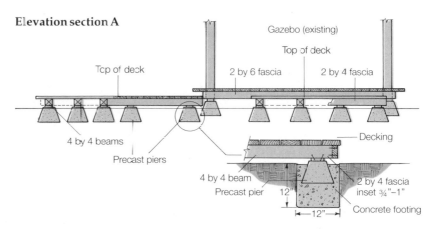

- Gazebo (existing)
- Top of deck
- Top of deck
- 2 by 6 fascia
- 2 by 4 fascia
- 4 by 4 beams
- Decking
- Precast piers
- 4 by 4 beam
- Precast pier
- 12"
- 2 by 4 fascia inset ¾"–1"
- Concrete footing
- 12"

FLOATING FREE

I designed this simple perennial-bordered platform to be a remote gathering place floating in a larger garden plan. Access to this urban getaway is via a flagstone path past herb and vegetable gardens.

Design: Jeffrey Miller, Landscape Architect

The simplicity of this deck allows it to float amidst the various garden areas within a small city yard. Since it faces south, it affords a place in the sun; because it is at the rear of the property, it affords a quiet retreat. The corner bench provides a place for conversation, sunning, reading, or, with the addition of a small table, a spot for dining.

To Adapt This Plan

This plan is readily adaptable. Consult the span charts on page 21 when enlarging the overall size. If you decide to run the decking parallel to either of the benches, the foundation will work as planned. By using a ledger, the deck can be attached to your house or other structure; by lengthening the posts and adding a skirt below the fascia, it can accommodate a small slope. Because this plan is small, compact, and self-sufficient, it can be built in almost any situation.

Building Notes

A simple rectangle cut short at 45 degrees on two sides, this deck is easy to build. The entire substructure is a series of 2 by 8 joists and fascia, nailed to posts on precast piers and connected to one another at either 90° or 45°. The bench support posts are nailed to 2 by 8 bracing between joists.

One concrete footing is poured as a support beneath the step; the step's supporting frame is hung from the deck fascia on joist hangers.

Step detail

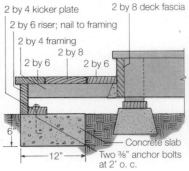

2 by 4 kicker plate

2 by 6 riser; nail to framing

2 by 4 framing

2 by 8

2 by 6

2 by 6

2 by 8 deck fascia

6"

12"

Concrete slab

Two ⅜" anchor bolts at 2' o. c.

Lay decking on the diagonal and be sure to bring the boards flush to the bench posts. To simplify this step, cut the deck boards to fit before putting the bench seat on (but after the bench posts are in place). Drop the deck boards down

over the bench posts. Alternatively, cut the deck boards so that there is a joint at the bench posts. Just add the bench seat and access step, and the deck is finished.

MATERIALS LIST*

Use pressure treated lumber for structural members, Clear Green redwood for visible members, and galvanized hardware.

Lumber

Posts	4 by 4
Joists/Blocking	2 by 8
Decking	2 by 6
Trim/Fascia	2 by 8
Step	2 by 4 kicker plate
	2 by 6 riser, tread
	2 by 8 tread
Bench	2 by 4 posts, fascia, seat boards, blocking beneath seat
	2 by 8 seat boards, blocking beneath decking

Masonry

Piers	Precast concrete
Cement	3' by 12" by 6"-deep stair footing

Hardware

Nails	16d box, for post to pier decking, seat boards
	16d finish, for mitred fascia
	1¼" joist hanger nails
Bolts	⅜" anchor, at kicker plate
Connectors	2 by 8 joist hangers for 90° and 45°

Finishes   Clear water sealant

*To determine the amount of materials needed for your deck, consult the guide on page 26.

Plan view

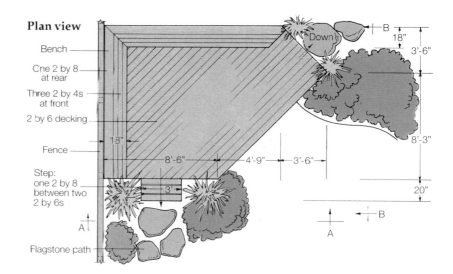

Bench
One 2 by 8 at rear
Three 2 by 4s at front
2 by 6 decking
Fence
Step: one 2 by 8 between two 2 by 6s
Flagstone path
Down
18"
3'-6"
8'-3"
8'-6" 4'-9" 3'-6"
20"
18"
3"
A
B

Deck framing

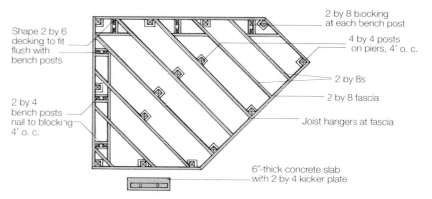

Shape 2 by 6 decking to fit flush with bench posts
2 by 4 bench posts nail to blocking 4' o.c.
2 by 8 blocking at each bench post
4 by 4 posts on piers, 4' o.c.
2 by 8s
2 by 8 fascia
Joist hangers at fascia
6"-thick concrete slab with 2 by 4 kicker plate

Bench framing at seat height

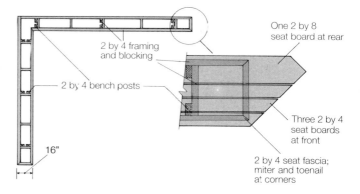

2 by 4 framing and blocking
2 by 4 bench posts
16"
One 2 by 8 seat board at rear
Three 2 by 4 seat boards at front
2 by 4 seat fascia; miter and toenail at corners

Elevations A & B

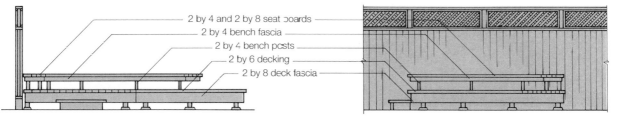

2 by 4 and 2 by 8 seat boards
2 by 4 bench fascia
2 by 4 bench posts
2 by 6 decking
2 by 8 deck fascia

LEAN & HANDSOME

To avoid a "boat dock" effect, this plan employs a modified octagon in its seating area. A seamless diagonal surface makes it seem larger than it is.

Design: David Kirk, CR, CGR; The Kirk Company

Tucked against one corner of the house, this clean-lined deck uses a built-in planter-bench to echo the form of an angular bump-out. This projection increases the deck's square footage by about a third, while intruding very little into the garden.

Laying decking on the diagonal creates an illusion of spaciousness, but also requires more lumber. And here, because the deck is small enough, there are no spliced boards. To enhance the sleekness of the design, all wood surfaces were sanded to a smooth finish, then stained to match the residence doors.

Lighted, boxed-in trees provide evening drama.

To Adapt this Plan

This deck is ideal for a house with simple lines on a flat lot. Its low level and tidy fascia float it neatly over a lawn. Although tucked into an L-shaped area here, the design would have the same slick effect across the straight back of a house, in a side yard, or at an entry.

To maintain the lean, seamless look, do not enlarge the plan beyond the length of available lumber. If you want to conserve lumber and reduce the amount of mitering, joists may be run perpendicular to the ledger, though the pattern made by the screws in the diagonal decking will no longer be at a 90° angle.

MATERIALS LIST*

Use pressure-treated lumber for structural members, surfaced Clear All Heart redwood or cedar for visible members, and galvanized hardware.

Lumber

Joists	2 by 6
Ledgers	2 by 6
Decking	2 by 6
Trim	2 by 2 nosing over 2 by 6 joist headers
Planter/Bench	2 by 4, 2 by 8 for legs; 2 by 6 for fascia, blocking, seat; 2 by 2 for siding; 2 by 4 for bracing, caps

Masonry

Piers	Precast concrete

Hardware

Nails	16d box for structure
Screws	3" for decking; ¼" lag screws for ledger

Preservatives

Preservatives	Protective pigmented coating; 6-millimeter plastic for planter liners

*To determine the amount of materials needed for your deck, consult the guide on page 26.

Building Notes

Deck screws were used for easy maintenance. Buy galvanized hardware: uncoated iron will stain redwood, and the tannic acid in redwood will deteriorate coated fasteners.

A nosing of 2 by 2 caps all decking edges, improving both durability and aesthetics. Line planters with 6-millimeter plastic, slit the bottom for drainage, and fasten the liner to the top edge of the planter before installing the 2 by 4 cap. To permit easy transplanting and prolong the life of the wood, use seasonal plants in pots. Cut a 2 by 6 to sit atop bricks or blocks inside the chamber; conceal voids with sphagnum moss.

Plan view of framing, foundation & decking

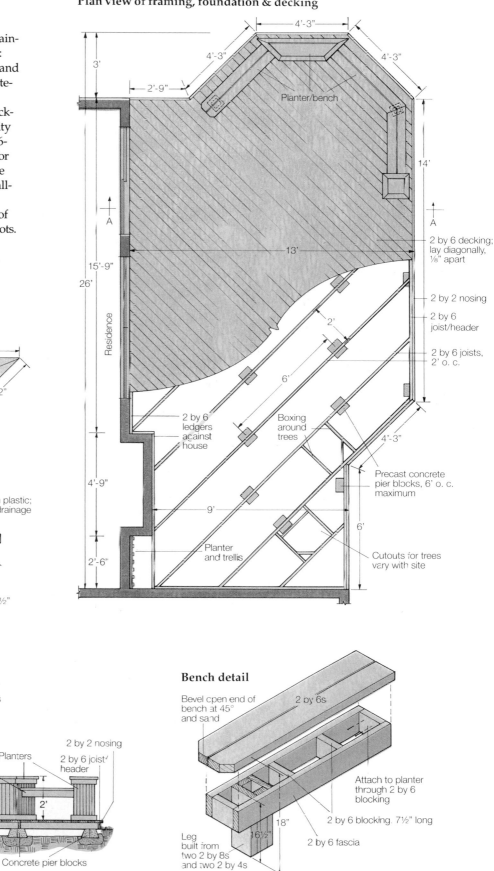

Trapezoid planter detail

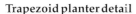
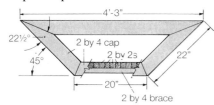

Square planter detail

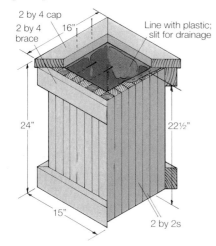

Elevation A

Bench detail

SPACE-SAVING ANGLE

The diagonal deck takes advantage of the largest dimension of the yard and provides a privacy-planting area in front of the master bedroom, ensuring leafy seclusion on both sides.

Design: Ann Christoph, ASLA, Landscape Architect

MATERIALS LIST*

Use pressure-treated lumber for structural members, surfaced redwood for visible members, and galvanized hardware.

Lumber

Posts	4 by 4
Beams	4 by 8
Joists	2 by 6
Blocking	2 by 6 atop beams and ledgers and sandwiched at bench and rail posts
Ledgers	4 by 8 for deck; 2 by 4 for benches
Decking	2 by 6
Fascia	2 by 8
Stairs	2 by 12 stringers; 2 by 6 treads; 2 by 4 risers
Railings	4 by 4 posts; 2 by 6 cap, rails, handrail; 2 by 4 stretchers; 1½" dowel
Bench	4 by 4 posts; 2 by 6 seat, fascia; 2 by 4 bracing, block (ripped); 2 by 2 trim

Masonry

Piers	12" precast concrete
Concrete	18" by 18" by 8" pier footings; 18" by 6' by 12" deep stair footing

Hardware

Nails	16d common nails or deck screws, countersunk and plugged; or brass screws
Bolts	⅝" bolts for ledgers and sand-wiched blocking; ½" bolts at all other vertical connections to posts; washers and nuts throughout
Connectors	Post caps and anchors; angled joist hangers at beam to ledger; sloped hangers at top of stringers; 8" by 8" by 2" angles at foot of stringer; reinforcing angles at joists to posts, blocking; bolts per manufacturer

*To determine the amount of materials needed for your deck, consult the guide on page 26.

The diagonal orientation of this plan leaves space to plant on three sides, resulting in an outdoor room with foliage walls. It also provides the largest deck possible with the least intrusion into garden space.

To Adapt This Plan

Although it overlooks a small garden here, this design is equally comfortable in the woods, at the beach, or as an entry. Build it on any side of the house, at a corner, or nestled into an L. You could use this deck as an adult entertaining area, with the stairs leading down to a children's play space.

To change the length or width of the deck, add or subtract joists and adjust their length.

Height is easily adjusted by changing the size of the posts and the number of steps or size of the risers. Without the posts, this deck can be built just a step above garden level.

Building Notes

Using lots of metal connectors gives added strength (see Materials List).

Extend the bench fascia around the exposed ends and miter the corners. Before ripping the 2 by 4 block behind the backrest, check the angle to be sure it's comfortable. Round the inside corners of the rail cap for comfort. Rout out the back side of the handrail to create a finger grip.

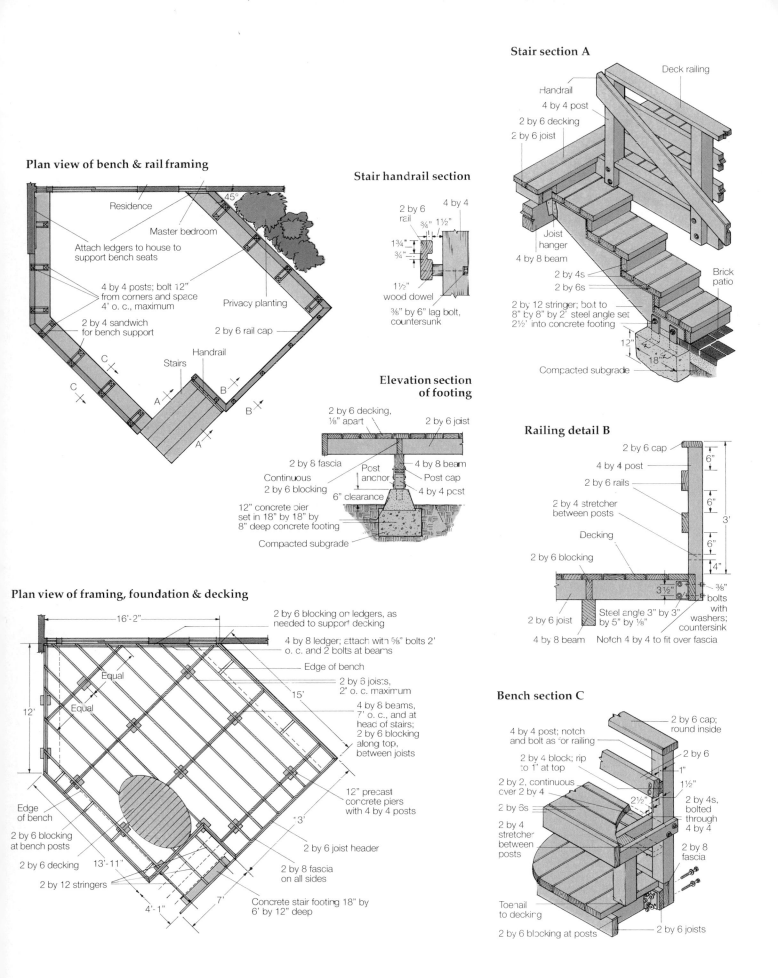

Plan view of bench & rail framing

Residence

45°

Master bedroom

Attach ledgers to house to
support bench seats

4 by 4 posts; bolt 12"
from corners and space
4' o. c., maximum

Privacy planting

2 by 4 sandwich
for bench support

2 by 6 rail cap

Handrail

Stairs

C

C

A

B

B

A

Stair handrail section

2 by 6
rail

4 by 4

¾" 1½"

1¾"

¾"

1½"

wood dowel

⅜" by 6" lag bolt,
countersunk

Elevation section
of footing

2 by 6 decking,
⅛" apart

2 by 6 joist

2 by 8 fascia

4 by 8 beam

Post
anchor

Post cap

Continuous
2 by 6 blocking

4 by 4 post

6" clearance

12" concrete pier
set in 18" by 18" by
8" deep concrete footing

Compacted subgrade

Plan view of framing, foundation & decking

16'-2"

2 by 6 blocking on ledgers, as
needed to support decking

4 by 8 ledger; attach with ⅝" bolts 2'
o. c. and 2 bolts at beams

Edge of bench

Equal

2 by 6 joists,
2' o. c. maximum

15'

Equal

4 by 8 beams,
7' o. c., and at
head of stairs;
2 by 6 blocking
along top,
between joists

12'

12" precast
concrete piers
with 4 by 4 posts

Edge
of bench

2 by 6 joist header

2 by 6 blocking
at bench posts

3'

2 by 6 decking

2 by 8 fascia
on all sides

2 by 12 stringers

13'-11"

4'-1"

7'

Concrete stair footing 18" by
6' by 12" deep

Stair section A

Deck railing

Handrail

4 by 4 post

2 by 6 decking

2 by 6 joist

Joist
hanger

4 by 8 beam

2 by 4s

2 by 6s

2 by 12 stringer; bolt to
8" by 8" by 2' steel angle set
2½' into concrete footing

Brick
patio

12"

18"

Compacted subgrade

Railing detail B

2 by 6 cap

6"

4 by 4 post

2 by 6 rails

6"

2 by 4 stretcher
between posts

3'

Decking

6"

2 by 6 blocking

4"

3½"

⅜"
bolts
with
washers;
countersink

2 by 6 joist

Steel angle 3" by 3"
by 5" by ⅛"

4 by 8 beam

Notch 4 by 4 to fit over fascia

Bench section C

4 by 4 post; notch
and bolt as for railing

2 by 6 cap;
round inside

2 by 6

2 by 4 block; rip
to 1" at top

1"

2 by 2, continuous
over 2 by 4

1½"

2 by 6s

2½"

2 by 4s,
bolted
through
4 by 4

2 by 4
stretcher
between
posts

2 by 8
fascia

Toenail
to decking

2 by 6 blocking at posts

2 by 6 joists

STREETFRONT STRATEGY

This low-maintenance design spares the home-owners deck repair. Decking is laid on edge to eliminate bowing, cupping, and the sight of nails.

Design: Nick Williams & Associates

If you want to gain usable space from a tiny front yard, this is your plan. In just over 350 square feet, it provides both a distinctive entry area (defined by a fence and a change in direction of the decking boards) and a planter-bordered entertaining or relaxing area.

Matching the siding and finish on the fence to the style of your house assures a fully integrated design.

To Adapt This Plan

This easy-to-build deck works best on a flat or gently sloped site. Although in the situation shown here it faces the street, you could locate it off any side of the house. Connect it to another exposure by building an engawa (see page 92), or wrap it around a corner to allow access from different rooms.

The divider fence might be used to separate adjacent spaces outside different rooms—to distinguish, say, the area off a family room from that off a bedroom.

You can use this deck to bridge low ground between the street and the front door (just lengthen the posts as needed). If your house is below street level, adding this entry apron will help lift it visually.

If privacy is a problem, you can fence around the entire deck (here, stone planters serving as low walls form a sufficient barrier from the street). If your house is masonry, consider building a matching wall instead of a wooden fence; you can frame the deck to go around its footings.

MATERIALS LIST*

Use pressure-treated lumber for structural members, surfaced redwood for visible members, and galvanized hardware.

Lumber

Posts	4 by 4
Beams	4 by 6
Joists	4 by 6
Ledgers	2 by 6
Decking	2 by 4, on edge
Fascia	2 by 10
Other	¼" exterior plywood shims

Masonry

Piers	14" precast concrete

Hardware

Nails	16d; 8d for decking
Bolts	⅜" lag screws for house ledgers; masonry anchors for stone planter ledgers
Connectors	Joist hangers, post anchors, post caps

*To determine the amount of materials needed for your deck, consult the guide on page 26.

Plan view of decking

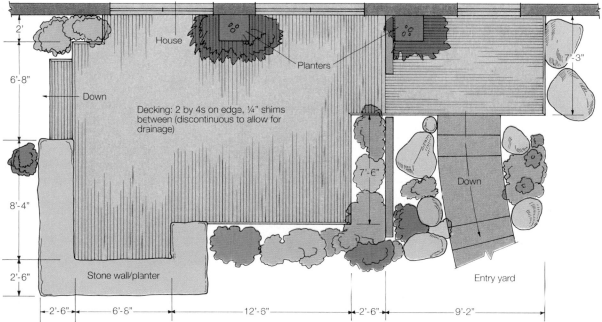

House

2'

6'-8"

Down

Decking: 2 by 4s on edge, ¼" shims between (discontinuous to allow for drainage)

Planters

7'-3"

8'-4"

7'-6"

Down

2'-6"

Stone wall/planter

Entry yard

2'-6" 6'-8" 12'-6" 2'-6" 9'-2"

Plan view of framing

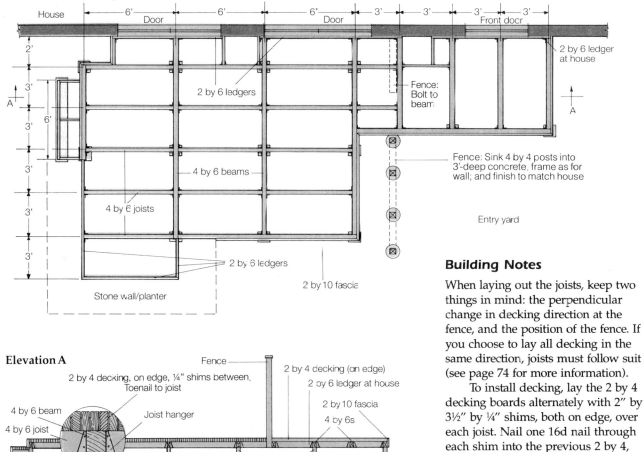

House 6' Door 6' Door 6' 3' 3' 3' 3' Front door

2'

2 by 6 ledger at house

A

3'

A

6'

2 by 6 ledgers

Fence: Bolt to beam

3'

Fence: Sink 4 by 4 posts into 3'-deep concrete, frame as for wall; and finish to match house

3'

4 by 6 beams

4 by 6 joists

Entry yard

3'

2 by 6 ledgers

2 by 10 fascia

Stone wall/planter

Elevation A

Fence

2 by 4 decking, on edge, ¼" shims between.
Toenail to joist

4 by 6 beam

4 by 6 joist

Joist hanger

Grade

4 by 4 posts

2 by 4 decking (on edge)

2 by 6 ledger at house

2 by 10 fascia

4 by 6s

Precast piers

Building Notes

When laying out the joists, keep two things in mind: the perpendicular change in decking direction at the fence, and the position of the fence. If you choose to lay all decking in the same direction, joists must follow suit (see page 74 for more information).

To install decking, lay the 2 by 4 decking boards alternately with 2" by 3½" by ¼" shims, both on edge, over each joist. Nail one 16d nail through each shim into the previous 2 by 4, then toenail the 2 by 4 with one 8d nail into the top of the joist.

DECK THE HILLS

My challenge, on a steep lot with an existing pool, was to increase the limited outdoor entertaining space and provide a comfortable place from which to enjoy an unusually scenic view.

Design: Peter Koenig, Landscape Designer

MATERIALS LIST*

Use pressure-treated lumber for structural members, All Heart redwood for exposed members, and galvanized hardware.

Lumber

Posts	4 by 4
Beams	4 by 6
Joists/Blocking	2 by 6
Decking	2 by 6
Fascia	2 by 6 at steps; 2 by 12 at straight sides; on curve, two 1 by 12s each milled to ½", laminated
Railings	Curved: three ⅜" by 4" benderboards, laminated
	Straight: 2 by 6 cap, 2 by 4 rail
	Both: 2 by 2 balusters
Other	2 by 6s cut 8" long, as blocks between footings and posts

Masonry

Concrete	Footings 12" by 12" by various depths

Hardware

Nails	16d box or common for framing; 8d box or common for decking; 8d concrete for footing blocks
Bolts	⅜" for bench posts and balusters

*To determine the amount of materials needed for your deck, consult the guide on page 26.

Situated just below the crest of the sloping back yard, this deck takes advantage of the scenery without obstructing the view from the house, which sits just uphill from the pool. The deck's level changes mimic those of the low foothills beyond. And its cantilevered projections out over the slope create a seating area from previously unusable space (see photo on front cover).

An important consideration here was to locate the new wooden decking adjacent to the concrete pool decking, yet far enough from the water so it would not be subject to the spotty bleaching and hastened deterioration bathers' splashes can cause.

To Adapt This Plan

The interesting angles and curves of this design would be attractive almost

anywhere—even if built on one level in a flat lot. This plan can be built on any slope, provided the footings meet local building codes. In a situation where the deck will be only a few inches above grade, you can set all the footings as shown in the foundation detail for flat areas (see page 42) and remove the railings.

For a large, flat deck, eliminate level changes and rely on changes in the diagonal decking pattern for visual interest.

The entire deck may be enlarged or made smaller, but for best design results, maintain the original proportions.

In a very large yard, try turning the plan around to face the house. On an upsloping hillside, the round part of the deck will be a promontory from which to view the rest of the garden.

Plan view

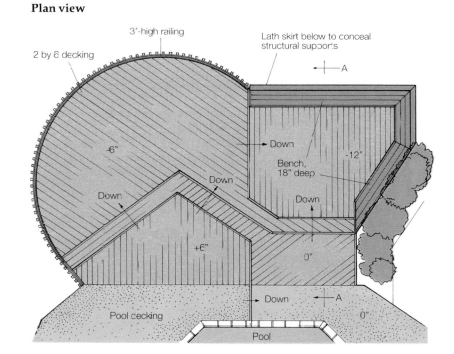

Foundation & framing

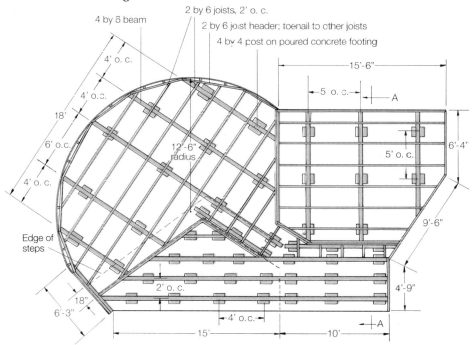

DETAILS

Building Notes

Begin by laying out the perimeter of the deck in order to make sure that your hillside can accommodate the plan. If not, adjust placement or size of the component decks.

Choose the longest straight joist line in each section and use it to determine the location of the piers. Use a construction level to set elevations.

Two tasks may require professional help. On steep slopes, pier holes should be drilled with an auger attached to a truck or tractor drilling rig. (Size and construction of piers and footings are a function of your soil conditions and total deck size.) And in any site, the curved railing and fascia should be laminated.

The table seen on the cover and on page 40 was not part of the original design. If you want to build a similar table, think of it as a large movable bench, and use the drawing of the bench section, below, as a guide. The table's surface matches the 2 by 6 decking boards; the side trim matches the step fascia (miter at the corners); and the legs match the bench posts, but are not bolted to the substructure. The outline of the tabletop follows the angles created by the benches.

Elevation section A

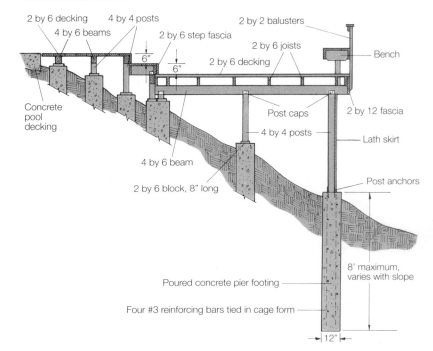

Foundation detail for flat areas

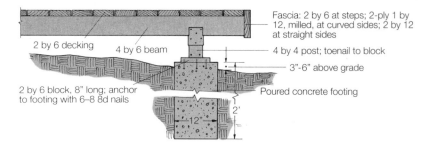

Bench & straight railing section

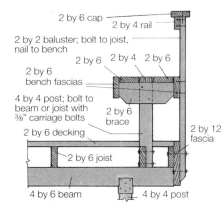

Curved railing section

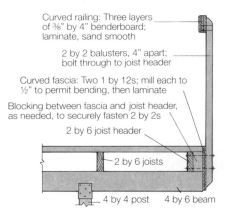

GARDEN PENINSULA

In this small city garden, a pair of narrow balconies reach out from the house for daylight and views. A circular, bench-lined peninsula extends into the yard as an outdoor gathering spot.

Design: Jeffrey Miller, Landscape Architect

This plan features three levels of decking: a railed upper balcony; a lower balcony that functions as an L-shaped covered walkway; and, three steps down, a circular platform with built-in seating. Stairs rise to the upper balcony and descend to the peninsula deck and garden below.

The use of geometry gives interest here, as the circular deck, with its trapezoidal seats, plays against the stacked, rectangular balconies.

To Adapt This Plan

This plan is suitable for any small back or side yard. It takes full advantage of a fine view.

To eliminate the upper balcony, just cut post heights to end beneath the wraparound deck's bench seats. You can continue the wraparound deck as far as necessary to locate the stairs more conveniently.

The width of the balconies can be adjusted to accommodate the width of

MATERIALS LIST*

Use pressure-treated lumber for structural members, Clear Green redwood for visible members, and galvanized hardware.

Lumber for circular deck

Posts	4 by 4
Joists	2 by 6
Blocking	2 by 6
Decking	2 by 4
Fascia	⅜" by 6" benderboard
Benches	⅜" by 4" benderboard fascia; 1 by 1 seat back ledger; 1 by 10 backs; 1 by 12 seat wedges; 2 by 4 posts, blocking; 2 by 6 cap

Lumber for first story

Posts	4 by 4
Joists	2 by 8
Ledgers	2 by 8
Decking	2 by 4
Fascia	2 by 8
Rail/bench	2 by 2 seat joists, seat slats, back slats; 2 by 4 back supports, seat fascia (front and back); 2 by 6 back slats, rail cap

Lumber for second story

Posts	4 by 4
Beams	2 by 12
Joists	2 by 10
Ledgers	2 by 10
Decking	2 by 4
Fascia	2 by 10
Railings	4 by 4 posts; 2 by 2 balusters; 2 by 4 top rail, end balusters; 2 by 6 cap

Lumber for all stairs

	2 by 12 stringers; 2 by 4 treads, kicker plate

Masonry

Piers	Precast concrete
Cement	12" by 12" by 18" second-story post footings; circular deck stair pad

Hardware

Nails	1¼" joist hanger nails; 8d finish for 1 by 1s; 10d finish for 2 by 2s; 16d box for 2 by 4s; 16d finish for 2 by 6 cap; 20d box for framing
Bolts	⅜" by 5" carriage for bench supports to posts; ½" by 8" carriage for second-story beam-post sandwich; ½" by 5" lag, with washers, at ledgers
Connectors	2 by 6, 2 by 8, 2 by 10 joist hangers; 4 by 4 post anchors
Finishes	Clear water sealant

*To determine the amount of materials needed for your deck, consult the guide on page 26.

your house. But do not increase their depth (distance from ledger to rail) or the cantilevering without consulting a licensed architect or engineer about the need for additional support.

The circular peninsula can be built larger, so long as you keep it in proportion to the balconies. If it were smaller, it might be impractical for entertaining or dining.

For clean lines and seamless-looking decking, keep the circular deck's diameter plus the width of the garden steps less than the length of the decking boards.

Building Notes

Locate your ledgers at the level of the first floor of the house. Then calculate how many steps you will need to reach the circular peninsula (and again, how many steps are needed between the peninsula and the garden). Locate the second-story ledger and calculate the height of your support posts from 6 inches above grade (top of footing with post anchor) to the top of this upper ledger.

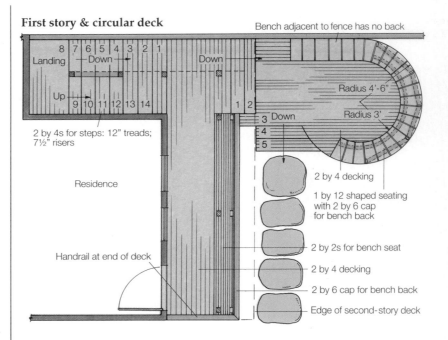

First story & circular deck

Bench adjacent to fence has no back

Landing — Down — Down

Up

9 10 11 12 13 14

2 by 4s for steps: 12" treads; 7½" risers

Residence

Handrail at end of deck

Radius 4'-6"
Radius 3'

Down

2 by 4 decking
1 by 12 shaped seating with 2 by 6 cap for bench back
2 by 2s for bench seat
2 by 4 decking
2 by 6 cap for bench back
Edge of second-story deck

Before building the staircase and landing to the upper balcony, extend decking surface of the walkway level around the corner of the house and all the way back under the landing and stair steps nine through twelve, creating a small, low deck for displaying plants or art and a storage area for toys or garden tools beneath steps one through seven.

First-story & circular deck framing

Second-story framing

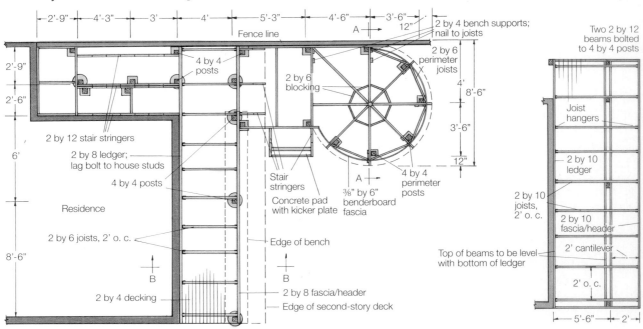

2'-9" — 4'-3" — 3' — 4' — 5'-3" — 4'-6" — 3'-6" — 12"

Fence line

A

2 by 4 bench supports; nail to joists

2'-9"

4 by 4 posts

2 by 6 perimeter joists

2'-6"

2 by 6 blocking

X

4'
8'-6"

3'-6"

2 by 12 stair stringers

2 by 8 ledger; lag bolt to house studs

6'

4 by 4 posts

Residence

Stair stringers

Concrete pad with kicker plate

⅜" by 6" benderboard fascia

A

4 by 4 perimeter posts

12"

2 by 6 joists, 2' o. c.

8'-6"

Edge of bench

B

B

2 by 4 decking

2 by 8 fascia/header

Edge of second-story deck

Two 2 by 12 beams bolted to 4 by 4 posts

Joist hangers

2 by 10 ledger

2 by 10 joists, 2' o. c.

2 by 10 fascia/header

2' cantilever

Top of beams to be level with bottom of ledger

2' o. c.

5'-6" — 2'

BENCH ON CIRCULAR DECK

Elevation section A

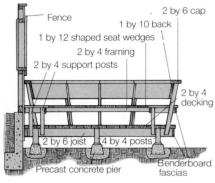

- Fence
- 2 by 6 cap
- 1 by 10 back
- 1 by 12 shaped seat wedges
- 2 by 4 framing
- 2 by 4 support posts
- 2 by 4 decking
- 2 by 6 joist
- 4 by 4 posts
- Precast concrete pier
- Benderboard fascias

Plan view of back support

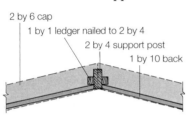

- 2 by 6 cap
- 1 by 1 ledger nailed to 2 by 4
- 2 by 4 support post
- 1 by 10 back

Bench with back

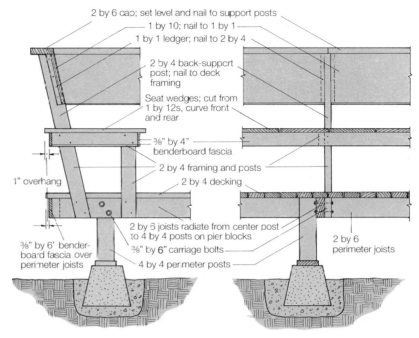

- 2 by 6 cap; set level and nail to support posts
- 1 by 10; nail to 1 by 1
- 1 by 1 ledger; nail to 2 by 4
- 2 by 4 back-support post; nail to deck framing
- Seat wedges; cut from 1 by 12s, curve front and rear
- ⅜" by 4" benderboard fascia
- 2 by 4 framing and posts
- 2 by 4 decking
- 1" overhang
- ⅜" by 6' benderboard fascia over perimeter joists
- 2 by 6 joists radiate from center post to 4 by 4 posts on pier blocks
- ⅜" by 6" carriage bolts
- 4 by 4 perimeter posts
- 2 by 6 perimeter joists

FIRST-STORY DECK DETAILS

Railing at end of deck

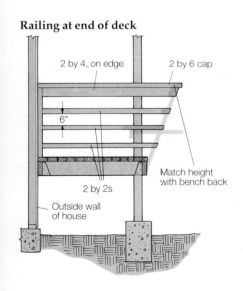

- 2 by 4, on edge
- 2 by 6 cap
- 6"
- Match height with bench back
- 2 by 2s
- Outside wall of house

Elevation section B

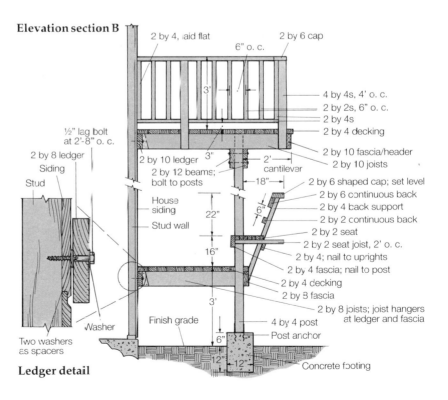

- 2 by 4, laid flat
- 6" o. c.
- 2 by 6 cap
- 3'
- 4 by 4s, 4' o. c.
- 2 by 2s, 6" o. c.
- 2 by 4s
- 2 by 4 decking
- 2 by 10 fascia/header
- 2 by 10 joists
- 2' cantilever
- 18"
- ½" lag bolt at 2'-8" o. c.
- 2 by 8 ledger
- Siding
- Stud
- 2 by 10 ledger
- 2 by 12 beams; bolt to posts
- House siding
- Stud wall
- 3"
- 22"
- 16"
- 6"
- 2 by 6 shaped cap; set level
- 2 by 6 continuous back
- 2 by 4 back support
- 2 by 2 continuous back
- 2 by 2 seat
- 2 by 2 seat joist, 2' o. c.
- 2 by 4; nail to uprights
- 2 by 4 fascia; nail to post
- 2 by 4 decking
- 2 by 8 fascia
- 3'
- 2 by 8 joists; joist hangers at ledger and fascia
- 4 by 4 post
- Post anchor
- Finish grade
- 6"
- 12"
- 12"
- Concrete footing
- Washer
- Two washers as spacers

Ledger detail

CAPTURING LOST SPACE

In a city side yard, squeezed between houses, interesting proportions, crisp lines, and overlapping materials and spaces make a handsome environment for a spa and shower.

Designer: Landscape Collaborative with Tom Paratore

An overhead arbor and a privacy screen seclude the partially shaded deck and spa area on which this plan focuses. A shower is ingeniously tucked between two studs in the house's exterior wall, with plumbing hidden inside the house; over the shower's drain, a wooden grate is fitted into the patio surface of concrete pavers. Planting vines to cling to the arbors will increase privacy at the spa.

Past this calm outdoor soaking area, the side yard terraces downhill in a series of interrelated planters, retainers, and paved patios that lead to a play yard and garden at the rear of the house.

Square corners appear throughout the design, rhythmically repeated in the spa, privacy screen, arbors, and wooden retaining walls. Detailing is in a tranquil Northwest/Japanese style.

Outdoor lighting at the steps and under the trees makes the spa suitable for nighttime use.

To Adapt This Plan

This plan is a wonderful solution for a narrow side yard. Although it was built on a slope here, it would also work well on a level lot.

Some obvious changes will be required, depending on the particular spa you choose: decking height, the size of the spa opening, and location of and access to spa equipment will all be determined by the spa model you use. But you should locate the spa in a quiet spot with easy access back into the house, and be sure that both your house and your neighbor's are high enough above grade at the site of the spa to ensure privacy for bathers.

The width of your side yard will determine the width of decks, patio areas, planting areas, and steps.

MATERIALS LIST *

Use pressure-treated lumber for structural members, Clear redwood for visible members (Construction Heart rough redwood where specified), and galvanized hardware.

Lumber

Posts	4 by 4 rough
Beam/joists	2 by 6
Ledgers	2 by 8
Decking	2 by 6
Fascia/skirt	2 by 6; 1 by 6 over 2 by 10 header at stair #4
Stairs	2 by 12 stringers; 2 by 6 treads; 2 by 4 risers, kicker plate
Retainers	2 by 8 cap; 2 by 6 rough sides
Arbors/screen	4 by 4 posts, rough; 2 by 4 beams; 2 by 3 rails; 2 by 2 lattice, screen, shower arbor ledger; marine plywood shower backboard in 2 by 2 frame

Masonry

Piers	12" precast concrete
Concrete	Length of stairs by 12" wide by 6" deep for stair footing; 12" cubes for retainer post footings
Gravel	Footings, shower grate drainage

Hardware

Nails	16d box; 16d finish for arbor 2 by 4s; 12d finish for arbor 2 by 3s; 10d finish for arbor 2 by 2s
Screws	⅜" by 6" lags, washers at ledgers
Connectors	Deck clips at spa surround; joist hangers
Other	Metal drain pan, pipe to sewer, shower head, handles, pipes

Preservatives

	Marine enamel, caulk for house siding near shower

*To determine the amount of materials needed for your deck, consult the guide on page 26.

Building Notes

Use Construction Heart rough redwood for all vertical elements, including stairs, retaining walls, posts, and some arbor uprights. All wood not visible is pressure-treated Douglas fir. Arbor fasteners are galvanized finish nails, which are less conspicuous than common nails and do not detract from the beauty of the wood.

You will have to follow the manufacturer's specifications for the spa's foundation and installation, but ideally, the top of the spa will be flush with your deck. Be sure to rehearse access to spa equipment and adjust joist locations, if necessary, before you build. Install extra joists and blocking for fastening purposes if you intend to miter the corners of the spa deck. Deck clips are specified around the spa to help provide a safe and clean walking surface for bathers, and Clear Green redwood is used for the same reason.

The shower head is set in a backboard of marine plywood that is framed with 2 by 2s and enameled an aquamarine color to match the spa. Be sure to caulk all holes in the shower

CAPTURING LOST SPACE

area and in the side of the house where ledgers are attached.

The privacy screen (see Elevation section B) is supported by 4 by 4 posts. Three 2 by 3s are set on edge between them and serve as stringers for the tightly spaced upright 2 by 2s. Note the pattern created by mixing two different lengths. The moon arbor over the spa shares two of the same posts; they should be cut after deck level is established and arbor and detail levels determined. Arbor beams sandwich the posts and are topped by two layers of 2 by 2s at intervals that open up toward the center. The shower arbor extends from one of these 2 by 4 beam sandwiches, continues across to the house, and rests on a 2 by 2 ledger. Additional 2 by 2s, laid crosswise, complete the job.

Elevation section A

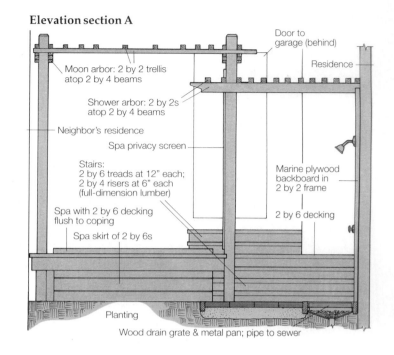

Moon arbor: 2 by 2 trellis atop 2 by 4 beams

Door to garage (behind)

Residence

Shower arbor: 2 by 2s atop 2 by 4 beams

Neighbor's residence

Spa privacy screen

Stairs:
2 by 6 treads at 12" each;
2 by 4 risers at 6" each
(full-dimension lumber)

Marine plywood backboard in 2 by 2 frame

2 by 6 decking

Spa with 2 by 6 decking flush to coping

Spa skirt of 2 by 6s

Planting

Wood drain grate & metal pan; pipe to sewer

Plan view of framing

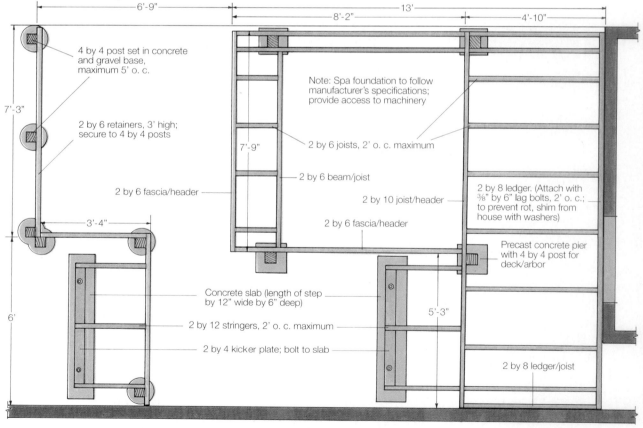

6'-9"

8'-2"

13'

4'-10"

4 by 4 post set in concrete and gravel base, maximum 5' o. c.

7'-3"

Note: Spa foundation to follow manufacturer's specifications; provide access to machinery

2 by 6 retainers, 3' high; secure to 4 by 4 posts

7'-9"

2 by 6 joists, 2' o. c. maximum

2 by 6 beam/joist

2 by 6 fascia/header

2 by 10 joist/header

2 by 8 ledger. (Attach with ⅜" by 6" lag bolts, 2' o. c.; to prevent rot, shim from house with washers)

2 by 6 fascia/header

3'-4"

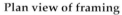

Precast concrete pier with 4 by 4 post for deck/arbor

6'

Concrete slab (length of step by 12" wide by 6" deep)

5'-3"

2 by 12 stringers, 2' o. c. maximum

2 by 4 kicker plate; bolt to slab

2 by 8 ledger/joist

Elevation section B

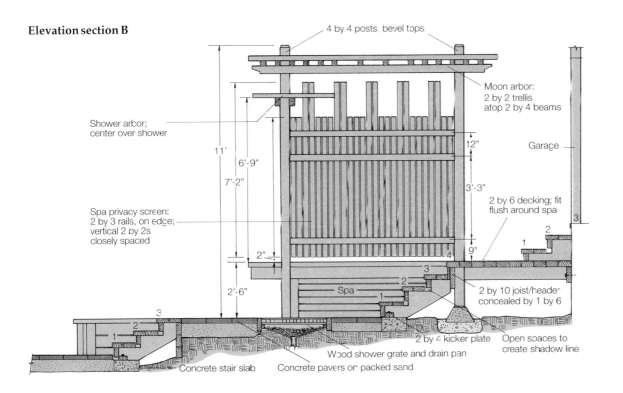

4 by 4 posts, bevel tops

Moon arbor:
2 by 2 trellis
atop 2 by 4 beams

Shower arbor;
center over shower

Garage

11'

6'-9"

7'-2"

12"

3'-3"

Spa privacy screen:
2 by 3 rails, on edge;
vertical 2 by 2s
closely spaced

2 by 6 decking; fit
flush around spa

2"

9"

4

3

2

1

2'-6"

Spa

2 by 10 joist/header
concealed by 1 by 6

3

2

1

3

2

1

2 by 4 kicker plate

Open spaces to
create shadow line

Concrete stair slab

Wood shower grate and drain pan

Concrete pavers or packed sand

Plan view with additions

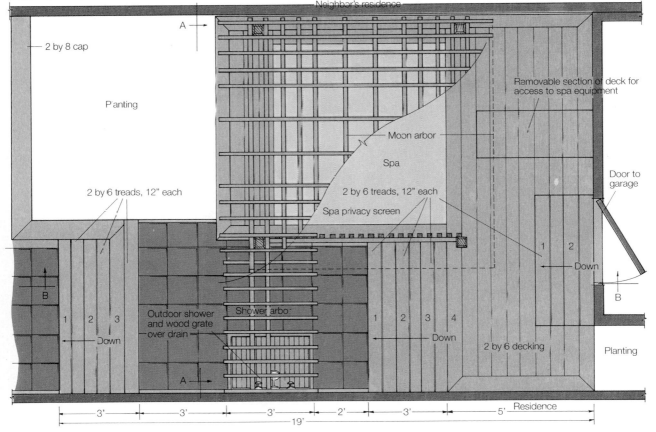

Neighbor's residence

A

2 by 8 cap

Removable section of deck for
access to spa equipment

Planting

Moon arbor

Spa

Door to
garage

2 by 6 treads, 12" each

2 by 6 treads, 12" each

Spa privacy screen

1

2

Down

B

B

1

2

3

Down

Outdoor shower
and wood grate
over drain

Shower arbor

1

2

3

4

Down

A

2 by 6 decking

Planting

3'

3'

3'

2'

3'

5'

Residence

19'

ON-STAGE SPA

To establish a major focal point in a fairly small garden and to provide privacy from adjacent neighbors, I angled this deck around the spa and shielded it with a screen that supports climbing vines.

Design: W. Jeffrey Heid, ASLA, Landscape Architect

Protective wings shelter this spa from both wind and neighbors and frame it like a theatrical stage. Low planters (extending barely 8 inches above the deck) and a continuous bench complete the design. Simple lines and symmetry create its clean look. Located across the lawn from the house, the deck draws the eye to the spa as the garden's focal point. No members of the deck are actually attached permanently to any part of the spa.

To Adapt this Plan

This plan is designed for a corner of a flat yard. You could use it on a gentle slope by adjusting the height of the posts. Since the tall screen has a wraparound effect, it is most successful when positioned facing the house. It could work along a side of a rear garden if the area itself were separated by a tall hedge, for example. Otherwise, the exposed side would reveal the back of the screen.

Size and shape of the deck will vary according to the spa you purchase. However, the basic shape can be adjusted quite simply; you can increase or decrease the entire deck to accommodate a larger or smaller spa, or use a different-sized spa within the dimensions shown. Remember to verify all dimensions and check electrical and plumbing access against manufacturer's instructions. If you change dimensions, refer to lumber span charts on pages 20–21.

Building Notes

Verify the dimensions of your new spa and map the deck and footing locations before beginning any excava-

Plan view of framing & foundation

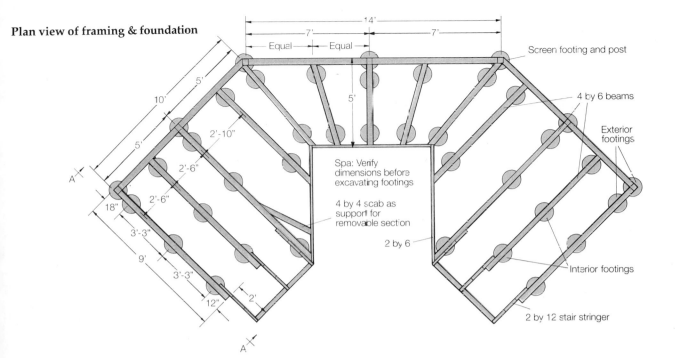

14'

7' | 7'

Equal | Equal

Screen footing and post

4 by 6 beams

Exterior footings

5'

10'

5'

2'-10"

2'-6"

2'-6"

18"

3'-3"

9'

3'-3"

12"

2'

5'

Spa: Verify dimensions before excavating footings

4 by 4 scab as support for removable section

2 by 6

Interior footings

2 by 12 stair stringer

A — A'

Interior footing

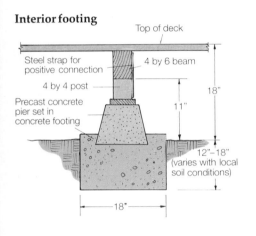

Top of deck

Steel strap for positive connection

4 by 6 beam

4 by 4 post

Precast concrete pier set in concrete footing

18"

11"

12"–18" (varies with local soil conditions)

18"

Decking section A

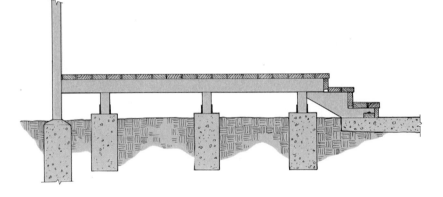

Exterior footing

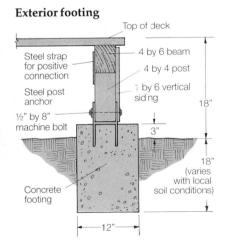

Top of deck

Steel strap for positive connection

4 by 6 beam

4 by 4 post

Steel post anchor

1 by 6 vertical siding

½" by 8" machine bolt

18"

3"

Concrete footing

18" (varies with local soil conditions)

12"

Stairs

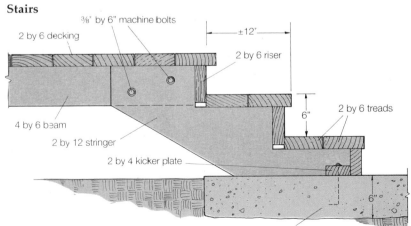

⅜" by 6" machine bolts

2 by 6 decking

±12'

2 by 6 riser

2 by 6 treads

4 by 6 beam

2 by 12 stringer

6"

2 by 4 kicker plate

Walkway as footing

6"

tion. Be sure to inset the front row of footings 12″ to avoid conflict with the stair stringers. Provide adequate drainage away from deck and spa.

Prepare a base for the spa—either a concrete slab or compacted rock. Make provisions for the electrical requirements of the spa: you may want to call in an electrician for this. Be sure that all work complies with local codes and that you have enough power. The size and location of your equipment access hatch will be determined by the design of your spa. Frame this removable portion of decking so that it rests upon surrounding

beams and install the handle flush in order to protect bare feet.

After the main portion of the deck is built, protect the insides of the 2 by 12 bottomless planter frame by nailing a waterproof liner under the 2 by 6 cap. Caulk the nail holes.

When bolting the exterior posts on each side of the deck into their bases, one of the bolts should be long enough to later accommodate the 1 by 6 fascia that will be applied below the decking. Remove the long bolt, apply the fascia board, and reinsert the bolt. Attach the top of the fascia to the side of the 4 by 6 beam with nails.

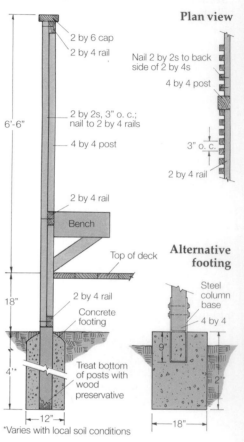

Elevation section B

Plan view

Alternative footing

Front elevation

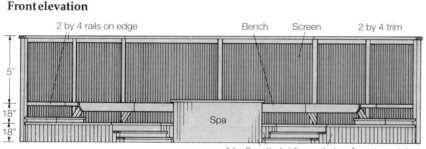

Plan view of decking

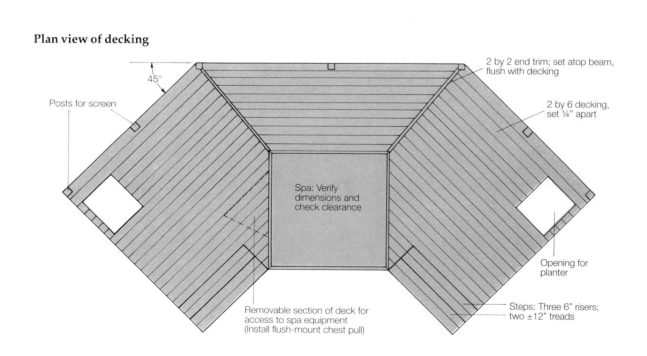

Section C: Planter details

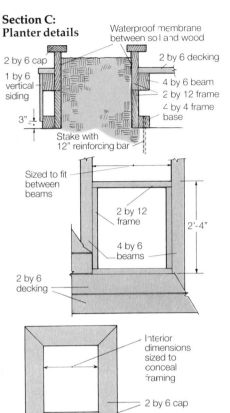

Waterproof membrane between soil and wood

2 by 6 cap

1 by 6 vertical siding

3"

Stake with 12" reinforcing bar

2 by 6 decking

4 by 6 beam

2 by 12 frame

4 by 4 frame base

Sized to fit between beams

2 by 12 frame

4 by 6 beams

2'-4"

2 by 6 decking

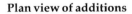

Interior dimensions sized to conceal framing

2 by 6 cap

MATERIALS LIST*

Use pressure-treated lumber for structural members, Construction Heart surfaced redwood for visible members, and galvanized hardware

Lumber

Posts	4 by 4 (redwood for screen; pressure-treated for deck)
Beams	4 by 6; 2 by 6 header
Decking	2 by 6; 2 by 2 trim
Siding	1 by 6
Stairs	2 by 12 stringers; 2 by 6 treads, risers; 2 by 4 kicker plates
Screen	2 by 6 cap; 2 by 4 rails, trim; 2 by 2 uprights
Planters	4 by 4 frame base; 2 by 12 frame; 2 by 6 cap
Benches	4 by 4 posts; 2 by 8 fascia; 2 by 4 braces, seat, trim; ¼" spacers

Masonry

Piers	Precast concrete

Concrete	18" by 18" by 12"–18" deep interior footings; 12" by 12" by 18" deep exterior footings; 12" by 12" by 48"deep screen footings or 18" by 18" by 24" deep screen footings; 6" deep stair footings

Hardware

Nails	16d for decking; 8d for 2 by 2s and trim
Bolts	½" by 8" machine bolts, washers, nuts at siding; ⅜" by 6" machine bolts, washers, nuts, at stair stringers
Connectors	Post anchors (exterior footings); steel straps (interior footings); column bases (alternative screen footings)
Other	Flush-mount chest pull for hatch; reinforcing bar

Preservatives

	Waterproof membrane for planter; wood preservative (post bottoms); two coats redwood sealer

*To determine the amount of materials needed for your deck, consult the guide on page 26.

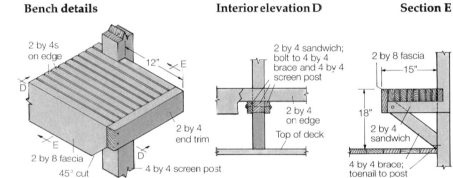

Bench details

2 by 4s on edge

12"

E

D

E

2 by 8 fascia

45° cut

2 by 4 end trim

4 by 4 screen post

Interior elevation D

2 by 4 sandwich; bolt to 4 by 4 brace and 4 by 4 screen post

2 by 4 on edge

Top of deck

Section E

2 by 8 fascia

15"

18"

2 by 4 sandwich

4 by 4 brace; toenail to post

Plan view of additions

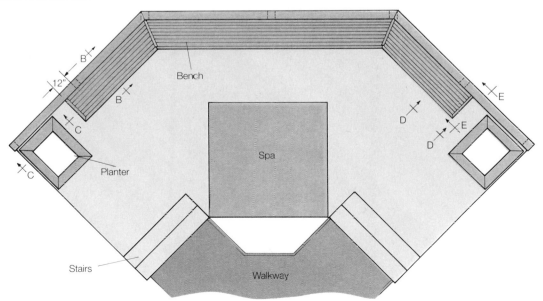

B

12"

B

C

C

Bench

Planter

Spa

D

E

D

E

Stairs

Walkway

DECK WITH A VIEW

Designed as a substantial outdoor living space, this deck takes advantage of a sunny exposure and fine outlook. The seating area steps down with the slope, preserving the view from the house.

Design: Robert Engman, AIA, Architect

Brilliant in its simplicity, this plan fashioned a large entertaining area from a narrow strip of land at the crest of a steep hill (see photo on page 4). An upper deck becomes a sofa seat for a lower deck; planters support the sofa's backrest; and armrest/end tables are a finishing touch.

The custom-designed table echoes the shape of the deck's front end. From the house, the diagonal decking directs the eye toward the planters and the view beyond.

To Adapt This Plan

If your lot goes uphill instead of down, or if your view is not appealing, turn the plan around. The lower deck will then be flush with your house's floor level and the built-in seating area will look back toward the house.

Here, the foundation is unusually hefty for two reasons: the site is in earthquake country, and the owners entertain very large groups. If soil conditions are questionable, subterra-

MATERIALS LIST*

Use pressure-treated lumber for structural members, surfaced Western red cedar for visible members, Clear Heart redwood for siding, and galvanized hardware.

Lumber

Posts	4 by 4
Beams	4 by 8
Joists	2 by 6 upper deck; 2 by 8 lower deck
Blocking	2 by 6 atop interior footings
Ledgers	2 by 8
Bracing	2 by 6 at stone wall
Decking	2 by 6
Fascia	1 by 8 (rail); 1 by 6 (sofa)
Interior stairs	2 by 12 stringers; 2 by 6 treads; 2 by 4 riser
Exterior step	4 by 12
Railings	4 by 4 post; 2 by 8 cap; 2 by 3 rail; trim ¾" by 2¼"
Planter/Sofa	2 by 8 armrest frame; 2 by 6 backrest; 2 by 4 frame, cap, armrest trim; 2 by 2 under cap; 1 by 8 siding; 1 by 6 fascia; ¾" plywood planter bottom, armrest top; ⅜" plywood planter interior sides; sheet-metal liner; 12" tiles; ¾" drainpipe; bitumen protective coating; all-weather cushions
Table	2 by 12 legs; 2 by 4 feet; ½" threaded rod brace; ¾" finish plywood top; waterproof membrane; granite top; ½" lag screws, washers

Masonry

Piers	See footing details
Concrete	Footings (all continuous): Perimeter and interior, 9" by 24" deep, includes 2 by 4 mudsill; stone wall, 2'-4" by 10" deep; 8" blocks (grout-filled); step, 6" by 15" deep
Gravel	Drain rock at perforated pipe

Hardware

Nails	16d
Bolts	⅝" at steps, post-to-rail; ½" anchors in interior footing, stone wall
Connectors	Post caps; #4 and #3 reinforcing bars; #3 stirrups; masonry anchors in stone wall
Other	½" copper pipe balusters; 4" perforated drainpipe at stone wall

*To determine the amount of materials needed for your deck, consult the guide on page 26.

Plan view of deck

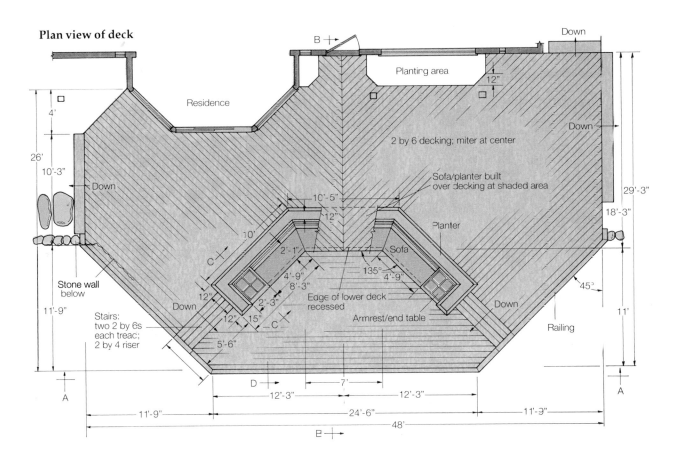

B

Down

Planting area

Residence

12"

Down

2 by 6 decking; miter at center

Sofa/planter built over decking at shaded area

Down

4'

26'

10'-3"

Down

10'-5"

12"

Planter

29'-3"

18'-3"

10'

Stone wall below

2'-1"

Sofa

135°

4'-9"

45°

C

4'-9"

8'-3"

Edge of lower deck recessed

11'

11'-9"

Stairs: two 2 by 6s each tread; 2 by 4 riser

12"

2'-3"

Down

Armrest/end table

Down

12"

15"

Railing

C

5'-6"

D

7'

A

A

12'-3"

12'-3"

11'-3"

11'-9"

24'-6"

48'

B

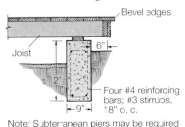

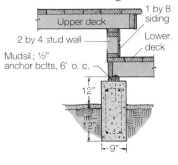

---

nean piers may be required beneath the continuous perimeter and interior footings. To determine the degree of support required at your site (and simplify foundation design if your circumstances permit it), consult a licensed architect or engineer.

Sofa height is determined by the relationship between deck levels. But you can alter the length or width of the decked area and contour its edge to suit the shape of your house.

To save money, you could buy ready-made cushions and tailor seat dimensions to fit them. You could also use ready-made planters. Granite table tops could be replaced by tile or other weatherproof surface. And in place of the custom-milled siding used by the architect, you could substitute standard tongue-and-groove or plain siding.

Building Notes

The planter/bench unit is not as complicated as it looks.

After you complete the two decks, measure 3½ feet back from

Perimeter footing

Bevel edges

Joist

6"

2'

9"

Four #4 reinforcing bars; #3 stirrups, 18" o. c.

Note: Subterranean piers may be required beneath footings where soil conditions are questionable. Anchor 12" into piers with two vertical #4 reinforcing bars.

Interior footing

1 by 8 siding

Upper deck

2 by 4 stud wall

Lower deck

Mudsill; ½" anchor bolts, 6' o. c.

12"

12"

9"

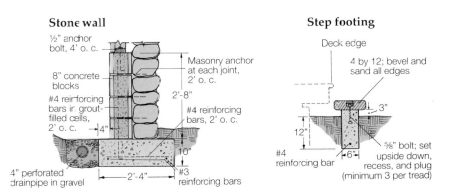

Stone wall

½" anchor bolt, 4' o. c.

Masonry anchor at each joint, 2' o. c.

8" concrete blocks

2'-8"

#4 reinforcing bars in grout-filled cells, 2' o. c.

4"

#4 reinforcing bars, 2' o. c.

10"

4" perforated drainpipe in gravel

2'-4"

#3 reinforcing bars

Step footing

Deck edge

4 by 12; bevel and sand all edges

3"

12"

6"

#4 reinforcing bar

⅝" bolt; set upside down, recess, and plug (minimum 3 per tread)

the outer edge of the upper one: this is the planter. Build planters (or install ready-made). Then construct 2 by 4 frames and attach to front side where the sofa back rest will be. Rip

braces, with their bases, at 12° (or any comfortable angle) from 2 by 6s (caps are ripped from 2 by 4s); nail to the frames and cover with three horizontal 2 by 6s. Frame and secure

the armrest/end tables at the ends of the backrest; top with ¾" marine plywood and tile.

Bring out some all-weather cushions, and you're set.

Elevation A

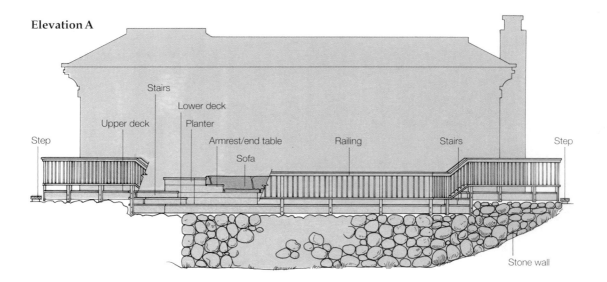

Plan view of foundation & framing

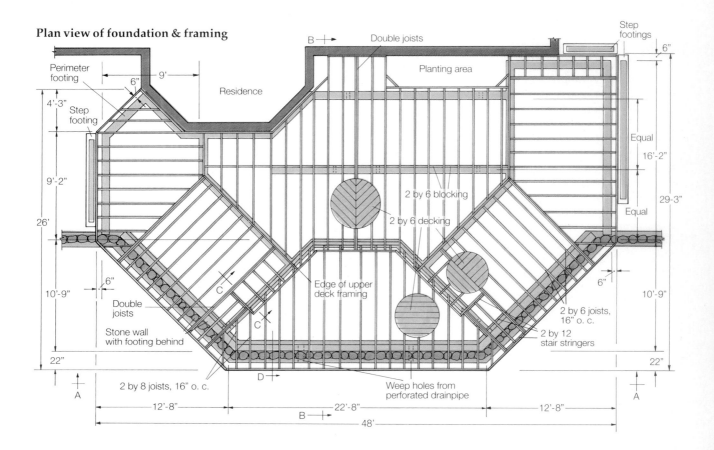

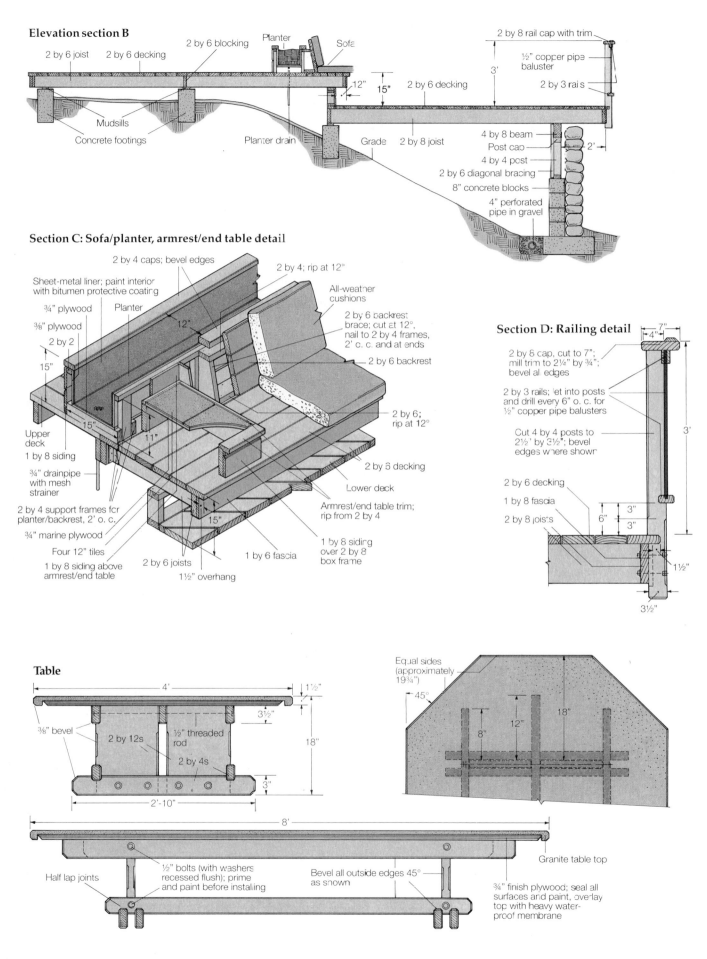

Elevation section B

2 by 6 joist
2 by 6 decking
2 by 6 blocking
Planter
Sofa
2 by 8 rail cap with trim
½" copper pipe baluster
3'
2 by 6 decking
2 by 3 rails
12"
15"
Mudsills
Concrete footings
Planter drain
Grade
2 by 8 joist
4 by 8 beam
Post cap
2'
4 by 4 post
2 by 6 diagonal bracing
8" concrete blocks
4" perforated pipe in gravel

Section C: Sofa/planter, armrest/end table detail

2 by 4 caps; bevel edges
2 by 4; rip at 12°
Sheet-metal liner; paint interior with bitumen protective coating
All-weather cushions
¾" plywood
Planter
2 by 6 backrest brace; cut at 12°, nail to 2 by 4 frames, 2' o. c. and at ends
⅜" plywood
12"
2 by 2
2 by 6 backrest
15"
2 by 6; rip at 12°
Upper deck
2 by 6 decking
1 by 8 siding
Lower deck
¾" drainpipe with mesh strainer
15"
11"
2 by 4 support frames for planter/backrest, 2' o. c.
Armrest/end table trim; rip from 2 by 4
¾" marine plywood
15"
Four 12" tiles
1 by 8 siding over 2 by 8 box frame
1 by 8 siding above armrest/end table
2 by 6 joists
1 by 6 fascia
1½" overhang

Section D: Railing detail

7"
4"
2 by 8 cap, cut to 7"; mill trim to 2¼" by ¾"; bevel all edges
2 by 3 rails; let into posts and drill every 6" o. c. for ½" copper pipe balusters
3'
Cut 4 by 4 posts to 2½' by 3½"; bevel edges where shown
2 by 6 decking
1 by 8 fascia
3"
2 by 8 joists
6"
3"
1½"
3½"

Table

4'
1½"
3½"
⅜" bevel
2 by 12s
½" threaded rod
18"
2 by 4s
3"
2'-10"
Equal sides (approximately 19¾")
45°
18"
12"
8"
8'
Half lap joints
½" bolts (with washers recessed flush); prime and paint before installing
Bevel all outside edges 45° as shown
Granite table top
¾" finish plywood; seal all surfaces and paint, overlay top with heavy water-proof membrane

PATIO PLATFORM

Our goal was to link the kitchen and the garden with a series of interconnected spaces. The upper deck leads to a lower deck, which sits just one foot above the patio and its arbor-covered nook.

Design: David and Robert Trachtenberg with Salo Rawet

This multilevel deck and stair system is an integration of elements that fit together like a carefully thought-out puzzle. A closer look reveals that decks become steps, steps become benches, benches become planters, and the entire structure frames and overlooks the charming brick patio.

A major factor in this particular design was weather. Though the arbor-shaded upper deck off the kitchen makes an attractive transition to the lower garden, this area is often too windy for comfort. But the conversation nook at patio level, with its matching arbor and lower position, is very sheltered and cozy.

The perimeter fence not only defines the property but also serves as backrest to the benches. Coordinating tables were built to complete this cohesive design (see page 93).

To Adapt This Plan

Though designed for a flat yard behind a house with an elevated first floor, this deck can be adapted to a variety of sites. A lot with a gentle downslope is also quite suitable.

You can use this plan to enclose any small space, providing privacy outdoors even in an urban neighborhood. Or align this deck to overlook a larger garden from its long side.

Some tailoring of dimensions is likely to be required. If your house is closer to ground level, eliminate a step or two as needed (the reverse, of course, is also true). You can easily shorten or extend the length or width of either the upper or lower deck, and

MATERIALS LIST*

Use pressure-treated lumber for structural members; surfaced Clear redwood for decking, planter caps, bench seats, and railing; rough redwood for all other visible members; and galvanized hardware.

Lumber

Posts	4 by 4
Beams	4 by 6
Joists/blocking	2 by 6, lowest landing only; 2 by 8; 2 by 12 header for upper deck
Ledgers	2 by 6 for lower deck and as header between brick and wraparound step; 2 by 12 at house
Decking	2 by 4
Fascia	2 by 12 upper deck; 2 by 4 lower deck
Stairs	2 by 4 framing under lowest wraparound step; 2 by 4 risers; 2 by 6 treads; 2 by 12 stringers
Railings	2 by 6 caps; 2 by 4 stringers; 2 by 2 pickets; 4 by 4 posts
Arbors	2 by 10 beams; 2 by 6 rafters, notched at beams; 2 by 4 rafters atop beams; 2 by 2s as top layer, patio arbor only; 4 by 4 posts
Benches	2 by 4 fascia, blocking; 2 by 6 seating; 4 by 4 posts
Planters	2 by 6 retainers/sides; 2 by 4 nailers at posts; 4 by 4 posts

Masonry

Piers	12" precast at corners (except at kitchen)
Concrete	All other footings (12" by 12" by 2')
Gravel	4" to 6" deep beneath footings and planters

Hardware

Nails	10d common for joists; 10d box for decking; 16d box for beam to pier blocks; 16d common for headers; 16d finish for visible vertical members, set in
Bolts	⅜" by 6" lags, with 4 washers each, at ledgers; ¼" bolts for post connections
Connectors	Joist hangers for 2 by 6, 2 by 8; nails as required

Preservatives

Caulk at ledger holes; felt paper lining in planters

*To determine the amount of materials needed for your deck, consult the guide on page 26.

Site plan with bench support

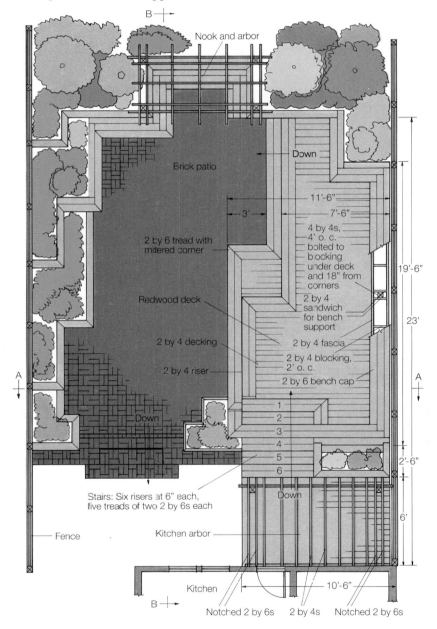

Nook and arbor

Down

Brick patio

11'-6"

3'   7'-6"

2 by 6 tread with mitered corner

4 by 4s, 4' o. c. bolted to blocking under deck and 18" from corners

2 by 4 sandwich for bench support

Redwood deck

2 by 4 decking   2 by 4 fascia

2 by 4 blocking, 2' o. c.

2 by 4 riser   2 by 6 bench cap

19'-6"

23'

Down

1
2
3
4
5
6

2'-6"

Down

Stairs: Six risers at 6" each, five treads of two 2 by 6s each

Fence

Kitchen arbor

6'

10'-6"

Kitchen

Notched 2 by 6s   2 by 4s   Notched 2 by 6s

turn the corner where it is most appropriate for your lot.

You can also adjust the size of the conversation nook by changing the lengths of the benches around its three sides. But be aware of the relationship between the levels: the benches are three risers above the main deck, and the planter tops are three risers above the benches.

Another possibility is to replace the brick of the original design with a third, lower level of decking. For continuity of design, run the boards in the same direction as the two existing decks.

Building Notes

All lumber used in the deck's substructure is pressure-treated. The designers of this plan feel that more scarce and costly woods should be conserved and used only where their beauty can be readily seen and appreciated.

Try to locate a structural member such as framing or the sill plate when attaching the ledger to the house. Predrill the ledger board every 3 feet on center, using a ⅜" bit for a ⅜" by 6" lag bolt. Predrill corresponding holes of a slightly smaller diameter into the exterior of the house. This will enable you to set the bolt securely without damaging or splitting the wall surface. Pack the holes in the house with clear silicone

Plan view of foundation, framing & bench support

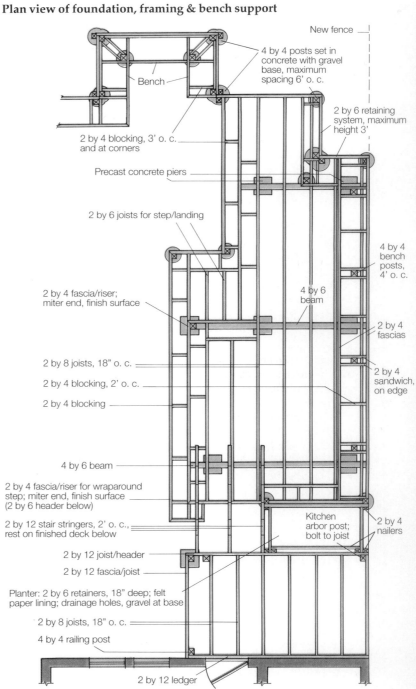

New fence

4 by 4 posts set in concrete with gravel base, maximum spacing 6' o. c.

Bench

2 by 6 retaining system, maximum height 3'

2 by 4 blocking, 3' o. c. and at corners

Precast concrete piers

2 by 6 joists for step/landing

4 by 4 bench posts, 4' o. c.

2 by 4 fascia/riser; miter end, finish surface

4 by 6 beam

2 by 4 fascias

2 by 8 joists, 18" o. c.

2 by 4 sandwich, on edge

2 by 4 blocking, 2' o. c.

2 by 4 blocking

4 by 6 beam

2 by 4 fascia/riser for wraparound step; miter end, finish surface (2 by 6 header below)

Kitchen arbor post; bolt to joist

2 by 4 nailers

2 by 12 stair stringers, 2' o. c., rest on finished deck below

2 by 12 joist/header

2 by 12 fascia/joist

Planter: 2 by 6 retainers, 18" deep; felt paper lining; drainage holes, gravel at base

2 by 8 joists, 18" o. c.

4 by 4 railing post

2 by 12 ledger

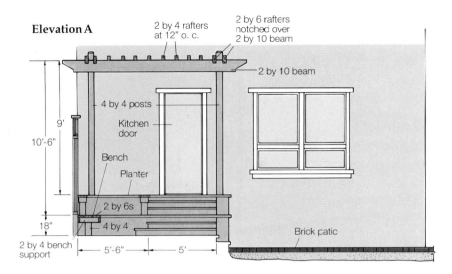

Elevation A

2 by 4 rafters at 12" o. c.

2 by 6 rafters notched over 2 by 10 beam

2 by 10 beam

4 by 4 posts

Kitchen door

Bench

Planter

2 by 6s

4 by 4

Brick patio

9'

10'-6"

18"

2 by 4 bench support

5'-6"

5'

for water protection. For each lag bolt, use one washer on the front of the ledger and two or three washers between ledger and house. Floating the ledger will protect the house from moisture and any future deterioration.

Note that 2 by 6s are used as stair treads in order to accentuate level changes. Many have mitered corners.

If you are building your fence at the same time, additional seat support can be cantilevered off the 4 by 4 fence posts by lining them up with the 4 by 4 bench posts. Sandwich both posts between common blocking beneath seat level.

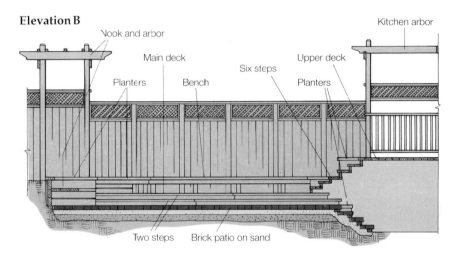

Elevation B

Nook and arbor

Kitchen arbor

Main deck

Upper deck

Six steps

Planters

Bench

Planters

Two steps

Brick patio on sand

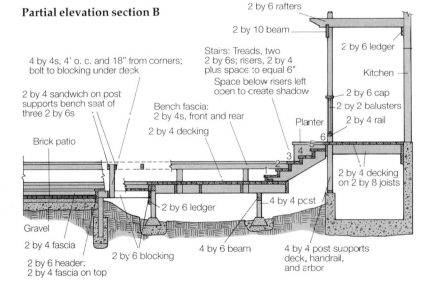

Partial elevation section B

2 by 6 rafters

2 by 10 beam

2 by 6 ledger

4 by 4s, 4' o. c. and 18" from corners; bolt to blocking under deck

Stairs: Treads, two 2 by 6s; risers, 2 by 4 plus space to equal 6"
Space below risers left open to create shadow

Kitchen

2 by 4 sandwich on post supports bench seat of three 2 by 6s

Bench fascia: 2 by 4s, front and rear

2 by 4 decking

Planter

2 by 6 cap

2 by 2 balusters

2 by 4 rail

Brick patio

6

5

4

3

2

2 by 4 decking on 2 by 8 joists

2 by 6 ledger

4 by 4 post

Gravel

2 by 4 fascia

2 by 6 header; 2 by 4 fascia on top

2 by 6 blocking

4 by 6 beam

4 by 4 post supports deck, handrail, and arbor

RECYCLED PATIO

We wanted to extend the living room into the rear garden. The need for shelter overhead influenced me to design a room-like deck enclosed by planters, a place where small children can safely play.

Design: Richard Rocha, Pilot Construction Company

In this plan, a dreary slab patio in a hot and sunny climate was decked over, expanded, and given shade with an overhead trellis.

The deck serves as an outdoor extension of the living room, a transitional area between living room and garden, a protected play space for young children, and a pleasantly shady place where their parents can sit or read outside.

The bench/planter units are kept low so as not to obstruct the view of the garden from the living room. They also bring flower color to eye level.

To Adapt This Plan

To build this deck on any level lot, use piers on footings every 8 feet on center. To build on top of an existing slab patio, anchor the beams (sleepers) to the concrete with steel straps or angles. (This plan uses both techniques because part of it is on the existing slab, part off.) If your patio already has an overhead, attach beams alongside its support posts with ½" machine bolts.

If the floor level of your house is well above grade, raise the deck by using posts on piers. Continue the siding all the way down to the ground to disguise the understructure.

For less shade, reduce or eliminate the 2 by 3s and fill in with a deciduous flowering vine. And for the feel of an old-fashioned enclosed porch, fasten screen panels between perimeter support posts.

Height and depth of benches may be adjusted for comfort. The seat continues under the backrest and be-

MATERIALS LIST*

Use pressure-treated lumber for structural members, surfaced redwood for visible members (rough lumber may be used for the overhead trellis), and galvanized hardware.

Lumber

Posts	4 by 4
Beams	4 by 8
Joists	2 by 8
Ledgers	2 by 8
Bracing	2 by 3
Decking	2 by 6
Trim/Fascia	¼" by 1½" lath at top, bottom, corners of planter sides and bottom of bench side; 1 by 4 at front of bench seat; 2 by 3 around trellis top; 2 by 6 sandwich at posts
Stairs	2 by 6 treads; 2 by 4 framing, blocking, risers; 1 by 4 trim
Trellis	4 by 4 posts; 4 by 8 header; 2 by 6 ledger, rafters; 2 by 3 trellis
Bench/Planters	2 by 6 seat deck, back; 2 by 4 cap; 2 by 3 framing; 1 by 6 tongue-and-groove siding
Gates	2 by 3 rails; 1 by 4 pickets

Masonry

Piers	12" precast concrete
Concrete	18" footings under piers; base for bricks

Hardware

Nails	16d common
Screws	⅜" by 5" at ledgers; brass wood screws for gate
Connectors	Joist hangers for rafters; post bases, caps; steel straps for beams-to-slab; bolts as required
Other	Hinges, latches, barrel bolts for gates
Finishes	Paint to match house trim

*To determine the amount of materials needed for your deck, consult the guide on page 26.

PLAN VIEWS

Overhead trellis

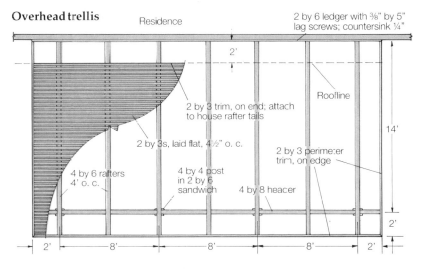

Residence

2 by 6 ledger with ⅜" by 5" lag screws; countersink ¼"

2'

Roofline

2 by 3 trim, on end; attach to house rafter tails

2 by 3s, laid flat, 4½" o. c.

2 by 3 perimeter trim, on edge

14'

4 by 6 rafters 4' o. c.

4 by 4 post in 2 by 6 sandwich

4 by 8 header

2'

2'   8'   8'   8'   2'

comes the planter bottom. Planter depth may be adjusted to accommodate container plants. For permanent planting, line planters with galvanized sheet metal or copper inserts. Provide drainage holes all the way down through the decking.

If you waterproof the area beneath the bench, it can be used to store toys, gardening gear, or seat cushions. Instead of nailing down a portion of a seat, construct a lift-up door; attach a frame to its underside and hinge it to the 2 by 6 planter wall. Be sure its ends rest securely on two 2 by 3 box frames below.

If you intend to paint your deck, use pressure-treated lumber instead of more costly surfaced redwood.

Building Notes

The steps are really one small pad atop another. Frame and block the lower step with 2 by 4s, then repeat the shape for the upper step, using smaller dimensions.

The rafters and header for the overhead can be corbelled and notched by using a band saw on wheels.

Be sure the trellis is square to the side of the house. Select 2 by 3s with good ends, since they will be visible from below. Set the 2 by 3 end trim so that its bottom is flush with the bottom of the other 2 by 3s. Plumb posts and header, then measure back to the ledger to establish the length of the rafters, extending them 2 feet beyond the notch.

If any decking boards have bad ends, conceal them beneath the bench. Save the best 2 by 6s for the bench seats and the center of the deck.

Gates have an uneven number of pickets, so curves will peak at the centers. To build them, screw pickets to rails (nails will quickly pull out with use), attach latch to center and hinges to ends, and then secure to planters.

Decking, benches, planters & stairs

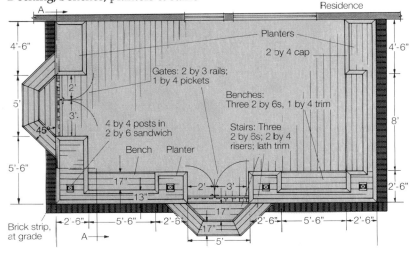

Residence

Planters

2 by 4 cap

4'-6"

4'-6"

Gates: 2 by 3 rails; 1 by 4 pickets

Benches: Three 2 by 6s, 1 by 4 trim

2'

8'

5'

4 by 4 posts in 2 by 6 sandwich

Stairs: Three 2 by 6s; 2 by 4 risers; lath trim

3'

45°

Bench   Planter

5'-6"

17"

2'   3'

2'-6"

13"

Brick strip, at grade

2'-6"   5'-6"   2'-6"

17"

2'-6"   5'-6"   2'-6"

A

17"

5'

Deck framing & foundation

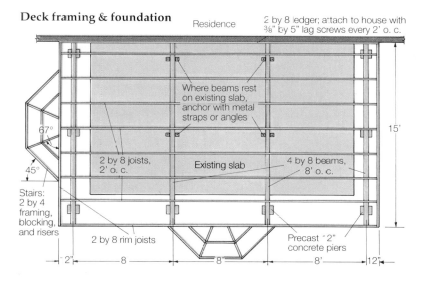

Residence

2 by 8 ledger; attach to house with ⅜" by 5" lag screws every 2' o. c.

Where beams rest on existing slab, anchor with metal straps or angles

15'

67°

45°

Stairs: 2 by 4 framing, blocking, and risers

2 by 8 joists, 2' o. c.

Existing slab

4 by 8 beams, 8' o. c.

2 by 8 rim joists

Precast 12" concrete piers

2'   8'   8'   8'   12"

DETAILS

Elevation section A

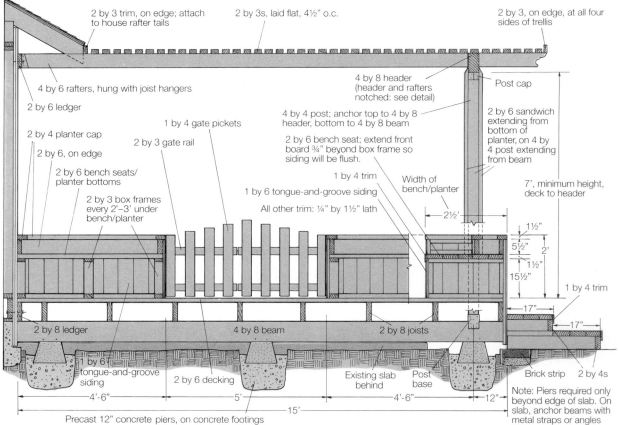

2 by 3 trim, on edge; attach to house rafter tails

2 by 3s, laid flat, 4½" o.c.

2 by 3, on edge, at all four sides of trellis

4 by 6 rafters, hung with joist hangers

2 by 6 ledger

4 by 8 header (header and rafters notched: see detail)

Post cap

2 by 4 planter cap

4 by 4 post; anchor top to 4 by 8 header, bottom to 4 by 8 beam

2 by 6 sandwich extending from bottom of planter, on 4 by 4 post extending from beam

2 by 6, on edge

1 by 4 gate pickets

2 by 3 gate rail

2 by 6 bench seat; extend front board ¾" beyond box frame so siding will be flush.

2 by 6 bench seats/ planter bottoms

1 by 4 trim

Width of bench/planter

7', minimum height, deck to header

1 by 6 tongue-and-groove siding

2 by 3 box frames every 2'–3' under bench/planter

All other trim: ¼" by 1½" lath

2½'

1½"
5½"   2'
1½"

15½"

1 by 4 trim

2 by 8 ledger

4 by 8 beam

2 by 8 joists

17"

17"

1 by 6 tongue-and-groove siding

2 by 6 decking

Existing slab behind

Post base

Brick strip

2 by 4s

Note: Piers required only beyond edge of slab. On slab, anchor beams with metal straps or angles

4'-6"

5'

4'-6"

12"

15'

Precast 12" concrete piers, on concrete footings

Overhead detail

Note: Notching is acceptable for decorative members only, never for decking or substructure

Notch bottom of rafter and top of header so both will be flush at top

2'

2'

4 by 6 rafter

Post cap

4 by 8 header

2 by 6s; bevel tops, nail to 4 by 4 posts

Bench/planter detail

2 by 4 caps

2 by 6 bench seat/planter bottom

2 by 6 tongue-and-groove siding

¼" by 1½" lath trim

1 by 4 trim at front of bench seat

2 by 6 decking

7"

15½"

Seat overhangs framing ¾" to be flush with siding

2 by 3 nailing plate between box frames

2 by 6 on edge

2'-6"

2 by 8 joists

Trellis support: 4 by 4 extends from beam; 2 by 6s extend from planter bottom

2 by 6 on edge

Planter

3'-4½"

¼" by 1½" lath

4 by 8 beam

1 by 6 tongue-and-groove siding

Box frames of 2 by 3s under bench/planter every 2'–3'

PLAYING THE ANGLES

This multilevel deck has three activity areas. The lower level lets entertaining and dining spread outward from the house. The upper level captures the small yard's only summer sun.

Design: Robert Mowat Associates

Extending across the full width of a small back yard, this deck meanders gracefully up a gentle slope. Wide steps zigzag uphill to handle the transition smoothly. Diagonal decking creates an illusion of greater space, and lush landscaping (the two central planters are built in) softens the design's angular contours (see photo on page 1).

To Adapt This Plan

Built for an upslope, this plan can easily be adapted for a downslope by reversing the direction of the steps so they lead down to the next level—which might overlook a dramatic view. Where the outlook is uninspiring, build the upper (rear) level a few steps higher, and it will itself supply a view.

Built on a single level, this plan would still gain visual interest from the directional changes of the decking and repeated use of angles.

Placing a privacy screen across the narrowest area could divide this large deck into two distinct smaller ones serving separate rooms.

Building Notes

Depth of footings will vary with soil conditions; check with your local building department.

To save wood, you can space joists farther apart (see page 21).

The arbor is optional. You might want to use it outside a large glass window or door to frame your view. The 3 by lumber of the original plan is custom-milled; to substitute 2 by lumber, place the posts 6 feet on center and adjust the spacing of the smaller battens between.

When finishing the bench seat, add fascia to all sides and miter the corners. Leave about ¼" between individual seat boards and between seat boards and fascia. Use brass wood screws to minimize clothing snags.

To build the planter, sink the posts into footings, nail exterior ply-

PLAYING THE ANGLES

Elevation section A

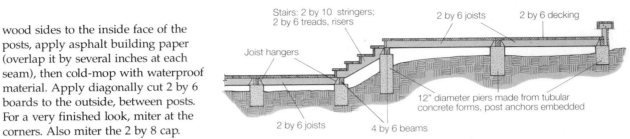

Stairs: 2 by 10 stringers; 2 by 6 treads, risers

Joist hangers

2 by 6 joists

2 by 6 decking

2 by 6 joists

4 by 6 beams

12" diameter piers made from tubular concrete forms, post anchors embedded

wood sides to the inside face of the posts, apply asphalt building paper (overlap it by several inches at each seam), then cold-mop with waterproof material. Apply diagonally cut 2 by 6 boards to the outside, between posts. For a very finished look, miter at the corners. Also miter the 2 by 8 cap.

MATERIALS LIST*

Use pressure-treated lumber for structural members, surfaced Construction Heart redwood (rough where specified) for visible members, and galvanized hardware.

Lumber

Beams	4 by 6
Joists	2 by 6
Decking	2 by 6
Stairs	2 by 10 rough stringers; 2 by 6 treads, risers
Arbor	6 by 6 rough posts; 3 by 8 rough beams; 3 by 3 rough battens

Planters	4 by 4 rough posts; 2 by 8 cap; 2 by 6 siding; 2 by 4 under cap; exterior plywood
Benches	4 by 4 rough posts; 2 by 12 rough retainers; 2 by 8 fascia; 2 by 6 rough blocking; 2 by 4 seats

Masonry

Concrete	Footings: 18" diameter by 2' deep for planters, arbor; 12" tube footings for deck (depth may vary); 12" by 3' by 6" deep pad for side stairs

Gravel	⅜" drain rock, 3" deep beneath footings and inside planter

Hardware

Nails	16d common
Screws	Brass wood screws for bench seat, fascia
Bolts	⅝", with washers, for arbor beams; ½", with washers, for seat posts
Connectors	Joist hangers; post anchors

Preservatives

	Asphalt paper, cold-mop waterproofing

*To determine the amount of materials needed for your deck, consult the guide on page 26.

Plan view

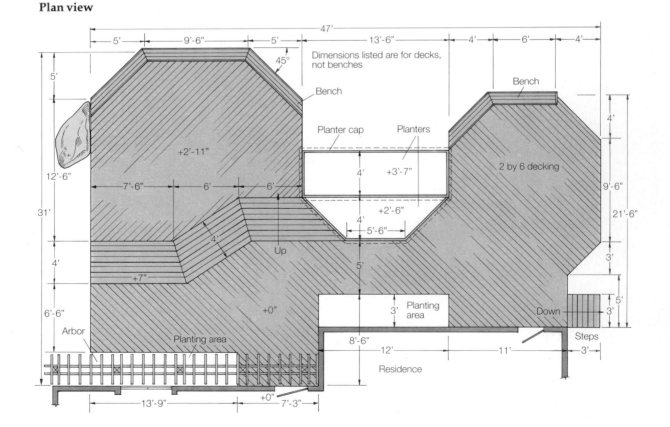

Planter detail

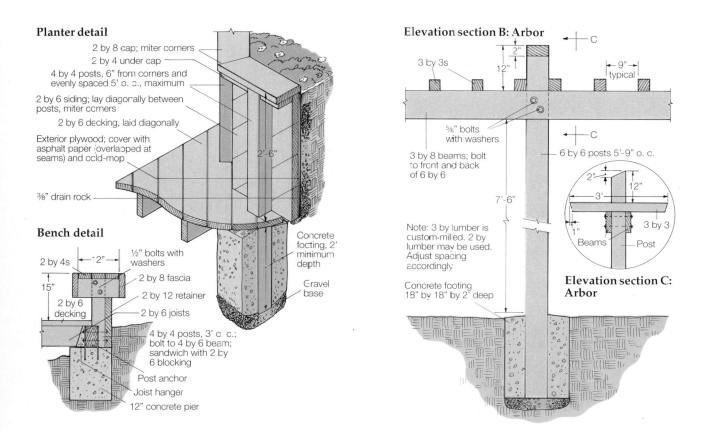

2 by 8 cap; miter corners

2 by 4 under cap

4 by 4 posts, 6" from corners and evenly spaced 5' o. c., maximum

2 by 6 siding; lay diagonally between posts, miter corners

2 by 6 decking, laid diagonally

Exterior plywood; cover with asphalt paper (overlapped at seams) and cold-mop

⅜" drain rock

2'-6"

Concrete footing, 2' minimum depth

Gravel base

Bench detail

2 by 4s

2"

15"

½" bolts with washers

2 by 8 fascia

2 by 12 retainer

2 by 6 decking

2 by 6 joists

4 by 4 posts, 3' o. c.; bolt to 4 by 6 beam; sandwich with 2 by 6 blocking

Post anchor

Joist hanger

12" concrete pier

Elevation section B: Arbor

C

3 by 3s

2"

12"

⅝" bolts with washers

3 by 8 beams; bolt to front and back of 6 by 6

C

9" typical

6 by 6 posts 5'-9" o. c.

2"

3'

12"

1"

3 by 3

Beams

Post

7'-6"

Note: 3 by lumber is custom-milled. 2 by lumber may be used. Adjust spacing accordingly.

Concrete footing 18" by 18" by 2' deep

Elevation section C: Arbor

Plan view of framing & foundation

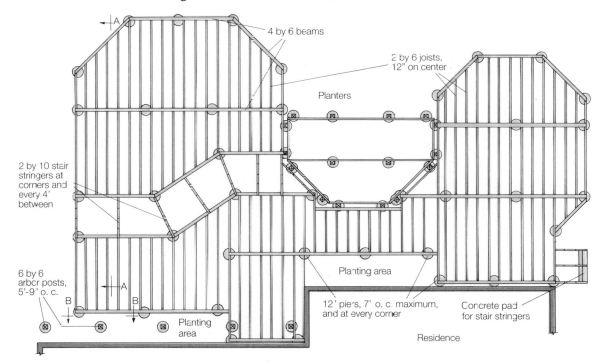

A

4 by 6 beams

2 by 6 joists, 12" on center

Planters

2 by 10 stair stringers at corners and every 4' between

6 by 6 arbor posts, 5'-9' o. c.

A

B

B

Planting area

Planting area

12' piers, 7' o. c. maximum, and at every corner

Concrete pad for stair stringers

Residence

DOUBLE-DECKER

To replace a cramped upper deck and inadequate concrete patio, I created a two-story deck—with 1,350 square feet of outdoor living space—plus a planting bed and two generous storage areas.

Design: Milt Charno & Associates

Based on a pattern of repeated angular bays, this deck system is a unified-looking complex made up of distinct subspaces.

In order to take maximum advantage of the space at ground level without making the lower deck disproportionately large, and to lend color and softness, a planting area was established, its form echoing the basic geometry of the decks. This enabled the designer to raise the grade, providing an interesting variety of levels and concealing an existing brick retaining wall along the side of the property.

One challenge of the project was to increase the square footage of the upper deck without having so many support posts that they would interfere with convenient use of the lower deck. The use of 6 by 6 posts allowed for longer spans between supports.

Stairs were positioned at a corner, saving space and tying the two levels together. This also meant that storage could be built under the stairs, as well as under the side of the upper balcony.

To Adapt This Plan

This deck was designed for a flat lot behind a two-story residence. But it could easily be built in a generous side yard.

If you live in a frost-free area, you will not need to have 4-foot-deep post holes but can use standard precast pier blocks on 12" by 12" by 12" deep concrete footings for the 4 by 4 posts and 12" by 12" by 18" deep concrete footings for the 6 by 6s.

The size of the deck can be modified according to the length of the back of your house and the depth of your lot. The upper deck should be built the size shown here or smaller; otherwise it could become too unwieldy, both visually and for its support system. And you don't want to have a forest of posts holding it up.

LOWER DECK

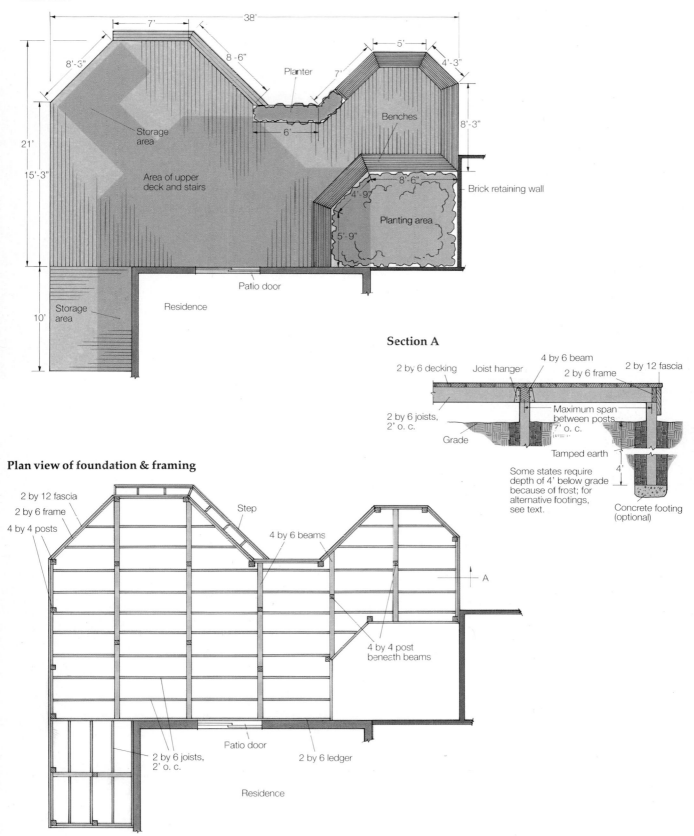

Plan view

7'
38'
8'-3"
8'-6"
Planter
7'
5'
4'-3"
Storage area
Benches
8'-3"
21'
6'
15'-3"
Area of upper deck and stairs
8'-6"
Brick retaining wall
4'-9"
Planting area
5'-9"
Storage area
Patio door
10'
Residence

Section A

2 by 6 decking · Joist hanger · 4 by 6 beam · 2 by 6 frame · 2 by 12 fascia

2 by 6 joists, 2' o. c.

Grade

Maximum span between posts 7' o. c.

Tamped earth

4'

Some states require depth of 4' below grade because of frost; for alternative footings, see text.

Concrete footing (optional)

Plan view of foundation & framing

2 by 12 fascia
2 by 6 frame
4 by 4 posts
Step
4 by 6 beams
A
4 by 4 post beneath beams
2 by 6 joists, 2' o. c.
Patio door
2 by 6 ledger
Residence

Add or subtract steps to adjust stair heights. Divide the total height by the number of steps to determine the size of the risers (see pages 82–83). Account for the landing in your calculations.

The fascia will change if your house is closer to grade than this one. You may have to reposition the planting area in relation to the door giving lower-deck access from the house.

MATERIALS LIST*

Use pressure-treated Southern pine (.40 retention) for structural members, Construction Heart redwood for visible members, cedar for storage siding, and galvanized hardware.

Lumber for upper deck

Posts	6 by 6
Beams	2 by 12 double joists
Joists	2 by 10
Ledgers	2 by 12
Decking	2 by 6
Fascia	2 by 12

Lumber for lower deck

Posts	4 by 4 (and at landing)
Beams	4 by 6
Joists	2 by 6
Ledgers	2 by 6
Decking	2 by 6
Fascia	2 by 12

Other lumber

Stairs	2 by 6 treads, risers; 2 by 12 stringers
Railings	2 by 6 cap; 2 by 4 rail, posts; 2 by 2 pickets
Storage	1 by 8 tongue-and-groove siding; 1 by 4 door brace
Benches	⅜" spacers; 2 by 4 slats, braces; 2 by 6 trim; 4 by 4 legs
Planters	1 by 4 braces; 2 by 6 siding; 2 by 4 cap

Masonry

Piers	Precast concrete (or see text, page 68)
Concrete	Footings in 4' post holes; for alternatives, see text
Gravel	Planter drainage

Hardware

Nails	8d finish for trim; 10d for framing and decking
Bolts	Anchor bolts at ledgers or ⅜" lags, washers, nuts
Connectors	2 by 6, 2 by 10, 2 by 12 joist hangers with nails
Other	Hinges, latches (storage)
Preservatives	Roofing paper for storage areas; waterproof lining for planters

*To determine the amount of materials needed for your deck, consult the guide on page 26.

Plan view of framing, decking, stairs & railing

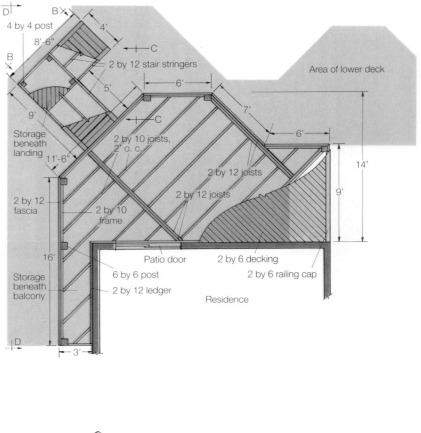

4 by 4 post · 8'-6" · 4' · C
2 by 12 stair stringers
Area of lower deck
5' · 6' · 7'
9' · 6'
Storage beneath landing
2 by 10 joists, 2' o.c.
14'
11'-6"
2 by 12 joists
9'
2 by 12 fascia
2 by 10 frame
2 by 12 joists
16'
Patio door · 2 by 6 decking
Storage beneath balcony
6 by 6 post
2 by 6 railing cap
2 by 12 ledger
Residence
3'

Elevation B: Railing detail

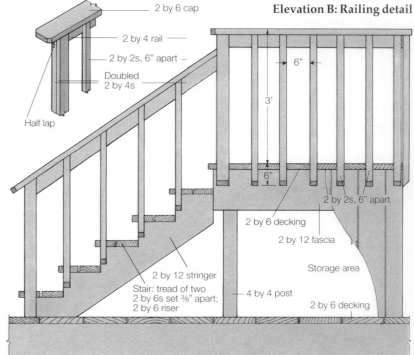

2 by 6 cap
2 by 4 rail
2 by 2s, 6" apart
Doubled 2 by 4s
Half lap
6'
3'
6'
2 by 2s, 6" apart
2 by 6 decking
2 by 12 fascia
Storage area
2 by 12 stringer
Stair: tread of two 2 by 6s set ⅜" apart; 2 by 6 riser
4 by 4 post
2 by 6 decking

Place benches where needed: close to the kitchen for entertaining, or under the spreading chestnut tree.

Building Notes

When building the benches, position pairs of 4 by 4 legs a maximum of 45 inches apart, evenly spaced between bench corners. Top each pair with a 2 by 4 brace. Place a line of ⅜" spacers between 2 by 4 slats at every brace and again midway between legs. Frame with mitered 2 by 6s on edge. To prevent tipping, either connect all benches to form one continuous expanse or toenail legs to decking.

It's easy to make the planters. Just build one side first, attaching 2 by 6s to 1 by 4 braces. Repeat for the other sides. Nail or screw 2 by 6s across both ends to form a box. Cap with the mitered 2 by 4 frame and toenail into place from the inside. Line with water-resistant material, provide drainage, and fill. Small planters can be used on the upper deck in summer, then, if necessary, stored in winter.

For storage areas, use the understructure of the stair landing and the balcony as starting points. Frame in walls and cover with tongue-and-groove siding. Provide an access door by attaching siding to a "Z" frame of 1 by 4s. The roof is the deck above. Remember to install roofing paper before decking these areas so what's stored below stays dry.

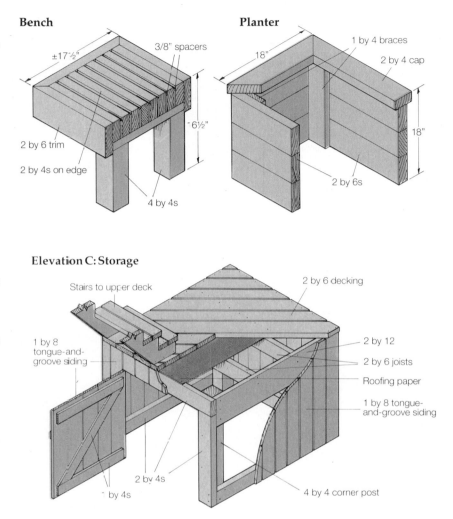

Bench

±17½"
3/8" spacers
2 by 6 trim
2 by 4s on edge
6½"
4 by 4s

Planter

18"
1 by 4 braces
2 by 4 cap
18"
2 by 6s

Elevation C: Storage

Stairs to upper deck
2 by 6 decking
1 by 8 tongue-and-groove siding
2 by 12
2 by 6 joists
Roofing paper
1 by 8 tongue-and-groove siding
2 by 4s
1 by 4s
4 by 4 corner post

Elevation D

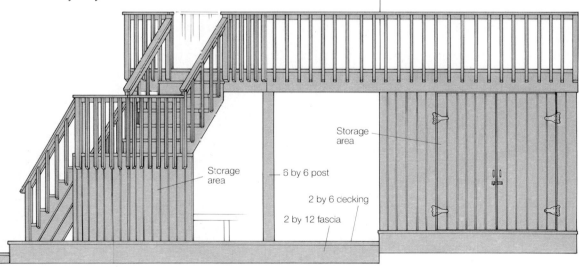

Storage area
Storage area
6 by 6 post
2 by 6 decking
2 by 12 fascia

FINISHING TOUCHES

In many situations, the totally unadorned deck is akin to a bare room: the space is defined, but "personality" has yet to be established. Only when it is fitted with railings, benches, planters, and such will the deck realize its full potential.

In this chapter we present an assortment of amenities to make your deck more inviting and more functional. Surface pattern and planters enhance its visual appeal. Benches and tables supply creature comforts and invite you to linger awhile. Screens, overheads, built-in lighting, and our special units are the extra touches that define the quality of your outdoor living space.

Railings and stairs are necessities for decks that float any distance above the ground. On pages 76–78 and 82–83, you will find a number of provocative variations on basic construction that individualize your solutions.

We have also included an engawa and a bridge to address two special situations: an engawa lets you extend a room outdoors; and a bridge enables you to make a pedestrian connection between two outdoor areas.

This all-in-one serving and entertainment unit is a handsome match for the owner-built redwood deck and house. For the plan, see page 95.

SURFACE PATTERN

Once you have selected a deck plan, you can turn to decorative considerations. First among these is the surface pattern created by the decking lumber. This pattern will establish your deck's "character," much as a wallpaper design gives ambiance to a room.

In many cases, a simple arrangement is the best choice: decking lumber set parallel, perpendicular, or diagonal to the deck's long axis. These simple patterns—in contrast to the more elaborate options such as the picture-frame and combination patterns illustrated below—create an illusion of size because the eye is drawn beyond the deck rather than encouraged to focus on design detail.

The most common—and most satisfactory—dimensions for decking lumber are 2 by 4 and 2 by 6. With smaller and larger boards, you run a greater risk of distortion from warping, twisting, or cupping. The simplest patterns employ boards in just one of these standard dimensions. But you can create a more richly textured look by combining boards of different widths in repeated sequences, such as 2 by 6s alternating with 2 by 3s or 2 by 4s. The examples below show several possibilities.

More elaborate patterns can be effective if you coordinate them with other surface textures or if they relate meaningfully to the architecture of your house. A basket-weave deck pattern, for example, might be a logical outdoor extension of an indoor parquet floor. A deck tucked into a corner of a house could employ opposing diagonal units that come together to

Parallel

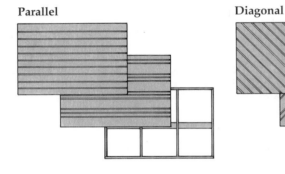

Diagonal

Basket weave

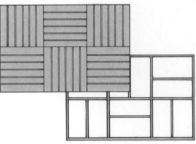

Herringbone

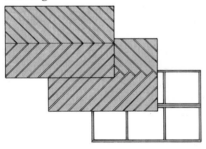

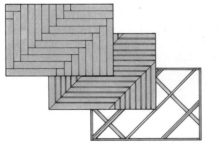

Picture-frame

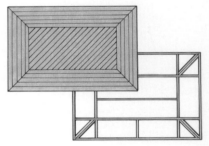

Bull's-eye

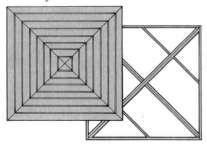

Combination

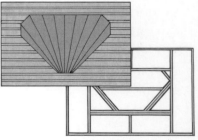

form a square "eye." But a herringbone deck surface interposed between, say, a shingled house and flagstone walkway would introduce an unrelated and unsettling distraction. In this case, the simple pattern created by parallel boards would provide a smooth and unobtrusive transitional surface.

The pattern of the surface lumber will, to some degree, determine the placement of support members in the deck's substructure. A diagonal pattern requires setting joists closer together; more elaborate designs call for doubling joists at regular intervals to permit nailing of abutting lumber. Which species of wood you use also affects the spacing of structural members. For more detailed information on these and other matters affecting spacing of supports, see the span charts on pages 20–21.

If your deck will be longer than the greatest length of standard decking lumber (generally 20 feet), you must plan how to handle abutting end joints. Of the two possibilities shown below, the pattern made by alternating individual boards is more subtle; by alternating groups of boards, you establish a design that calls attention to itself.

Whatever pattern you choose, allow about ¼" between boards for drainage, ventilation, and expansion and contraction of wood.

Abutment patterns

Alternating   Grouped

ACCOMMODATING NATURE

Think twice before you cut down a large tree or remove an intrusive boulder. Instead, consider how your deck might be enhanced by including such natural features as elements in your plan.

There are two approaches to building around a tree or rock. The simplest is to build a joist frame, then lay decking to the edge of it. A bit trickier, though involving the same substructural frame, is to make a custom-fitted cutout. Whenever you surround a tree with decking, remember two rules. First, allow space for the trunk to enlarge as the tree ages. And second, never attach lumber to the trunk: the tree's movement in wind will damage the deck. If you allow a generous opening, you can incorporate a bench into the plan, providing seating that's pleasantly tree-shaded.

A "built-in" rock or boulder will appear most natural if you cut the decking so that the boards follow its contours. As illustrated, scribe the rock's outline onto deck lumber butted against it. When all the affected boards are marked, cut along the lines, then secure the boards to the deck in the same order as they were marked. For examples, see pages 24, 27, and 34.

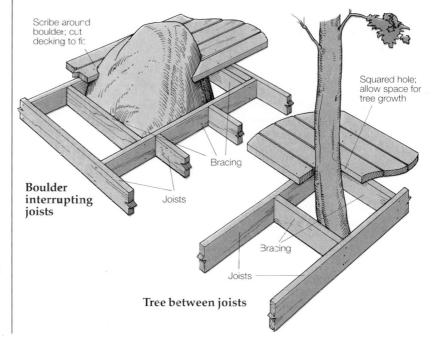

Scribe around boulder; cut decking to fit

Squared hole; allow space for tree growth

Boulder interrupting joists

Bracing

Joists

Bracing

Joists

Tree between joists

RAILINGS

For any deck elevated 30 inches or more above grade, a railing is desirable—and probably required. Local building codes govern the height of deck railings and the spacing between vertical and horizontal members. In general, railings should rise 36 to 42 inches above the deck's surface, have no more than 6 inches between vertical members, and be able to support a sitting or leaning person.

In addition to providing safety, well-designed railings can greatly enhance a deck's appearance. They are, in essence, low fences, generally open in construction, though solid railings are sometimes built to provide privacy or wind protection, or to suggest an impassable barrier. The great variety in design options lets you coordinate railings with the architecture, detailing, and materials of your house or other structures nearby. The 12 railings illustrated on these three pages suggest a range of possibilities, from simple to intricate, both in design and construction.

To support your railings, choose one of the basic construction approaches shown at right. If deck posts are to be extended up through the deck from pier blocks or bolted to joists, it is essential that you design your railing before you construct the substructure. If railings are to be attached to a fascia, they can be added at any time. Spacing between posts is determined by the load to be borne. In turn, the length of these spans determines the size of the railing's cap. As a general rule, a 2 by 4 cap can span posts up to 4 feet apart, and a 2 by 6 member can cap posts with a 6-foot span.

Think of the gate as a module of railing mounted on hinges. By repeating the railing design in the gate, you achieve a "seamless" appearance in your deck's surround. Be sure to position a post at either side of the gate.

ATTACHMENTS

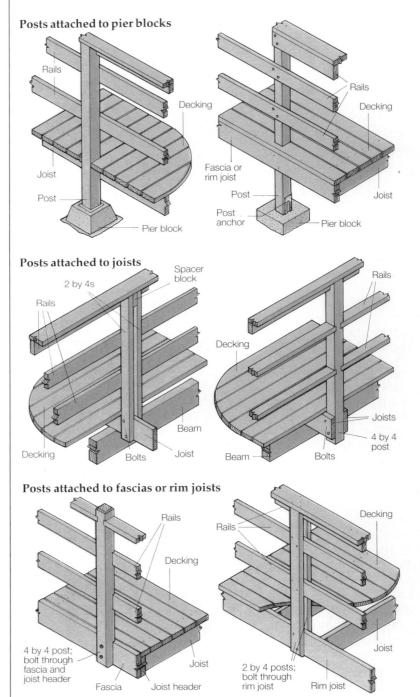

Posts attached to pier blocks

Rails
Decking
Joist
Post
Pier block

Rails
Decking
Fascia or rim joist
Post
Post anchor
Pier block
Joist

Posts attached to joists

2 by 4s
Rails
Decking
Bolts
Joist
Beam
Spacer block

Rails
Decking
Beam
Bolts
Joists
4 by 4 post

Posts attached to fascias or rim joists

4 by 4 post; bolt through fascia and joist header
Fascia
Joist header
Rails
Decking
Joist

Rails
Decking
2 by 4 posts; bolt through rim joist
Rim joist
Joist

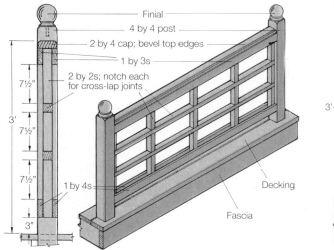

Finial
4 by 4 post
2 by 4 cap; bevel top edges
1 by 3s
2 by 2s; notch each for cross-lap joints
7½"
3'
7½"
7½"
1 by 4s
3"
Decking
Fascia

DESIGN: TOM WIRTH

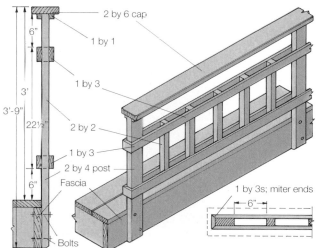

2 by 6 cap
1 by 1
6"
1 by 3
3'
3'-9"
22½"
2 by 2
1 by 3
2 by 4 post
6"
Fascia
Bolts
1 by 3s; miter ends
6"

DESIGN: JOHN HERBST, JR.

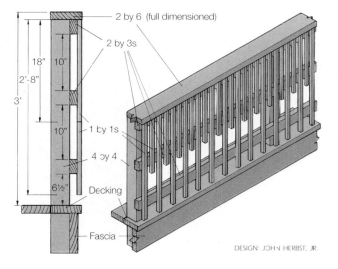

2 by 6 (full dimensioned)
2 by 3s
18"
10"
2'-8"
3'
10"
1 by 1s
4 by 4
6½"
Decking
Fascia

DESIGN: JOHN HERBST, JR.

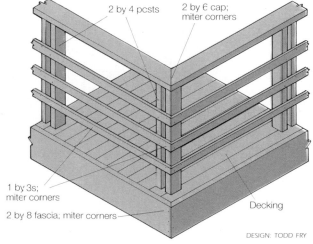

2 by 4 posts
2 by 6 cap; miter corners
1 by 3s; miter corners
2 by 8 fascia; miter corners
Decking

DESIGN: TODD FRY

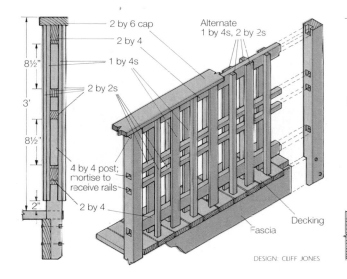

2 by 6 cap
2 by 4
1 by 4s
2 by 2s
Alternate 1 by 4s, 2 by 2s
8½"
3'
8½"
2"
4 by 4 post; mortise to receive rails
2 by 4
Decking
Fascia

DESIGN: CLIFF JONES

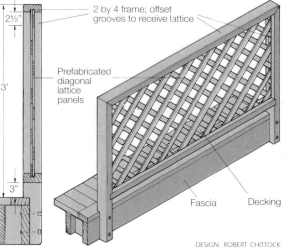

2 by 4 frame; offset grooves to receive lattice
2½"
Prefabricated diagonal lattice panels
3'
3"
Fascia
Decking

DESIGN: ROBERT CHITTOCK

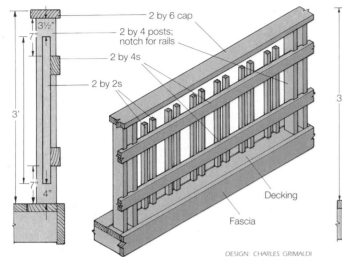

2 by 6 cap

2 by 4 posts; notch for rails

2 by 4s

2 by 2s

3½"

7"

3'

7"

4"

Decking

Fascia

DESIGN: CHARLES GRIMALDI

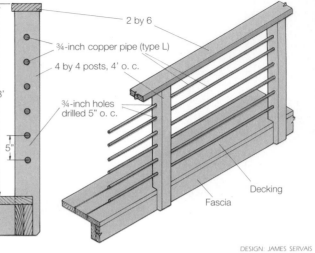

2 by 6

¾-inch copper pipe (type L)

4 by 4 posts, 4' o. c.

¾-inch holes drilled 5" o. c.

3'

5"

Decking

Fascia

DESIGN: JAMES SERVAIS

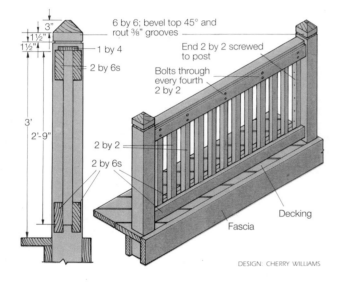

6 by 6; bevel top 45° and rout ⅜" grooves

1 by 4

2 by 6s

End 2 by 2 screwed to post

Bolts through every fourth 2 by 2

2 by 2

2 by 6s

3"

1½"

1½"

3'

2'-9"

Decking

Fascia

DESIGN: CHERRY WILLIAMS

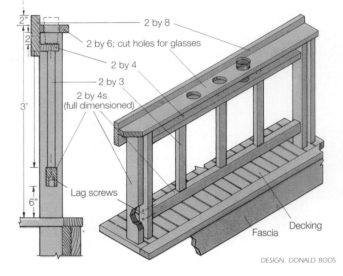

2 by 8

2 by 6; cut holes for glasses

2 by 4

2 by 3

2 by 4s (full dimensioned)

Lag screws

2"

2"

3'

6"

Fascia

Decking

DESIGN: DONALD BOOS

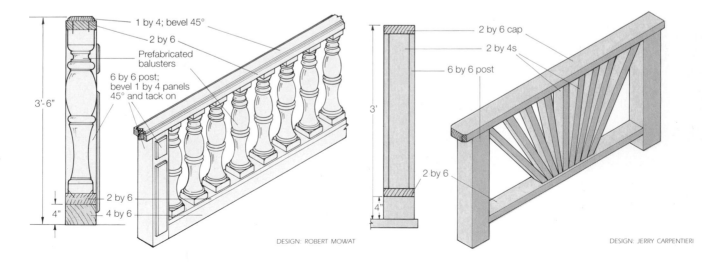

1 by 4; bevel 45°

2 by 6

Prefabricated balusters

6 by 6 post; bevel 1 by 4 panels 45° and tack on

2 by 6

4 by 6

3'-6"

4"

DESIGN: ROBERT MOWAT

2 by 6 cap

2 by 4s

6 by 6 post

2 by 6

3'

4"

DESIGN: JERRY CARPENTIERI

SCREENS

If you think of a screen as a tall railing, you'll easily grasp the construction fundamentals. However, their functions differ. Whereas a railing provides chiefly a physical barrier, a screen's purpose is to provide a visual or weather barrier—to block, moderate, or filter an objectionable view or breeze. Screens tend to be more solid or intricate than railings. But, like railings, the most attractive screens coordinate with existing structural elements. The drawings on this page and the next two pages illustrate both basic and elaborate patterns; you can use them singly or in combination.

Although screens don't need to bear the weight from leaning or sitting that railings must, their attachment to the deck should be no less

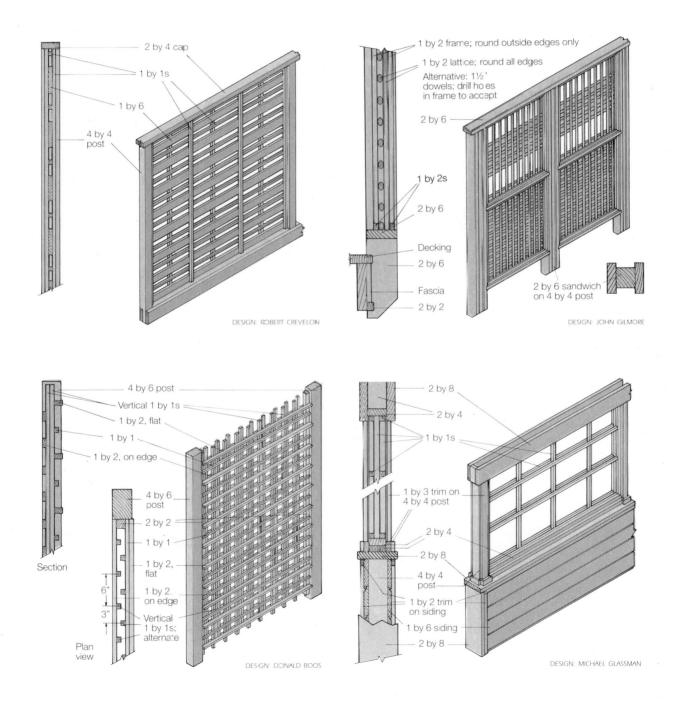

DESIGN: ROBERT CREVELON

DESIGN: JOHN GILMORE

DESIGN: DONALD BOOS

DESIGN: MICHAEL GLASSMAN

secure. Refer to the drawings on page 76 for three basic ways to establish a sturdy framework. The spacing of posts for screens is the same as that for railings: up to 4 feet apart if the cap is a 2 by 4, up to 6 feet if the cap is a 2 by 6. Maximum height for free-standing screens is 8 feet. Screens tied into other structures may be taller.

Hillside and upper-story decks may have a long-legged look because of the exposed support posts. If these structural members will be a visible part of your environment, you might want to construct a decorative "skirt" to mask them and, at the same time, visually anchor the deck to the ground. Such skirts are really screens that extend below (rather than above) deck level. You follow the same design guidelines as for screens; and skirts, like screens, are attached where the support posts are located.

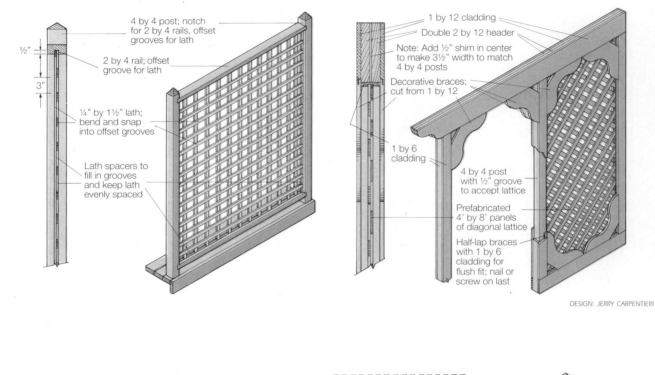

4 by 4 post; notch for 2 by 4 rails, offset grooves for lath

2 by 4 rail; offset groove for lath

½"

3"

¼" by 1½" lath; bend and snap into offset grooves

Lath spacers to fill in grooves and keep lath evenly spaced

1 by 12 cladding

Double 2 by 12 header

Note: Add ½" shim in center to make 3½" width to match 4 by 4 posts

Decorative braces; cut from 1 by 12

1 by 6 cladding

4 by 4 post with ½" groove to accept lattice

Prefabricated 4' by 8' panels of diagonal lattice

Half-lap braces with 1 by 6 cladding for flush fit; nail or screw on last

DESIGN: JERRY CARPENTIERI

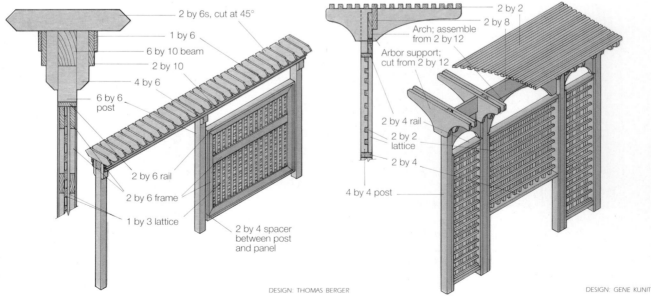

2 by 6s, cut at 45°

1 by 6

6 by 10 beam

2 by 10

4 by 6

6 by 6 post

2 by 6 rail

2 by 6 frame

1 by 3 lattice

2 by 4 spacer between post and panel

2 by 2

2 by 8

Arch; assemble from 2 by 12

Arbor support; cut from 2 by 12

2 by 4 rail

2 by 2 lattice

2 by 4

4 by 4 post

DESIGN: THOMAS BERGER

DESIGN: GENE KUNIT

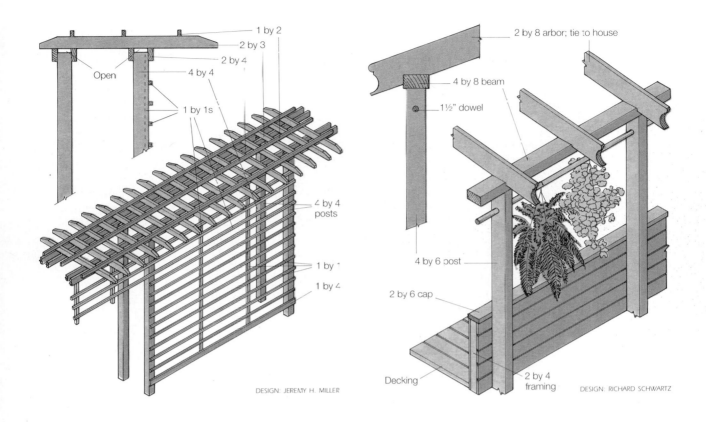

1 by 2

2 by 3

2 by 4

Open

4 by 4

1 by 1s

4 by 4 posts

1 by 1

1 by 4

DESIGN: JEREMY H. MILLER

2 by 8 arbor; tie to house

4 by 8 beam

1½" dowel

4 by 6 post

2 by 6 cap

Decking

2 by 4 framing

DESIGN: RICHARD SCHWARTZ

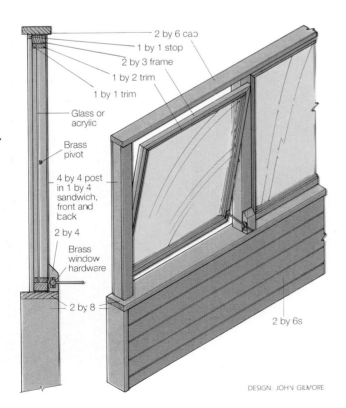

2 by 6 cap

1 by 1 stop

2 by 3 frame

1 by 2 trim

1 by 1 trim

Glass or acrylic

Brass pivot

4 by 4 post in 1 by 4 sandwich, front and back

2 by 4

Brass window hardware

2 by 8

2 by 6s

DESIGN: JOHN GILMORE

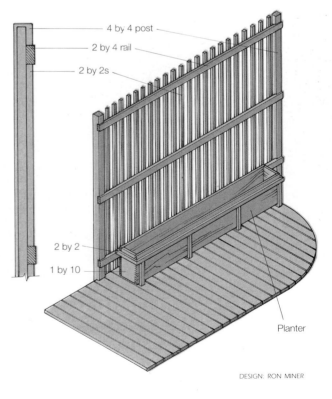

4 by 4 post

2 by 4 rail

2 by 2s

2 by 2

1 by 10

Planter

DESIGN: RON MINER

STEPS & STAIRS

Stairs are simply a means of making a comfortable transition from one level to another, one step at a time. If you have a low-level deck, its surface may be one easy step above the ground upon which it sits. But if the transition would feel awkward for the normal stride, you need to provide intermediate levels.

Comfort is the watchword for deciding the length of a stairway run and dimensions of the individual steps.

Step width. This depends on the anticipated traffic. For utility stairs, used by one person at a time, a 4-foot width is sufficient. Where two people might walk abreast, 5 feet is the minimum. Where more traffic is likely, increase the minimum step width by 2 feet per person.

Length of run. Mayan pyramids employ steps set in uninterrupted runs up dizzyingly steep slopes. To avoid creating your own "Mayan effect," figure that a single straight run of stairs should take in an elevation change no larger than 8 feet. If you need to make a greater ascent, interrupt the run of stairs with a landing. Changing the direction of ascent from the landing makes the climb seem less daunting and creates a more interesting design.

Step proportions. In step terminology, the flat surface on which you place your foot is the tread; the elevation difference between two treads is the riser. A workable rule of thumb for making comfortable steps is to be sure that the sum of the tread's depth plus double the riser's height equals 26 inches. Higher risers—more than 6½ inches—can be used for utility stairs, but shorter risers (and deeper treads) are preferable for general use. A minimum suggested tread depth is 9 inches, a maximum riser height 7½ inches.

Construction basics. Though all steps serve the same purpose, there are five

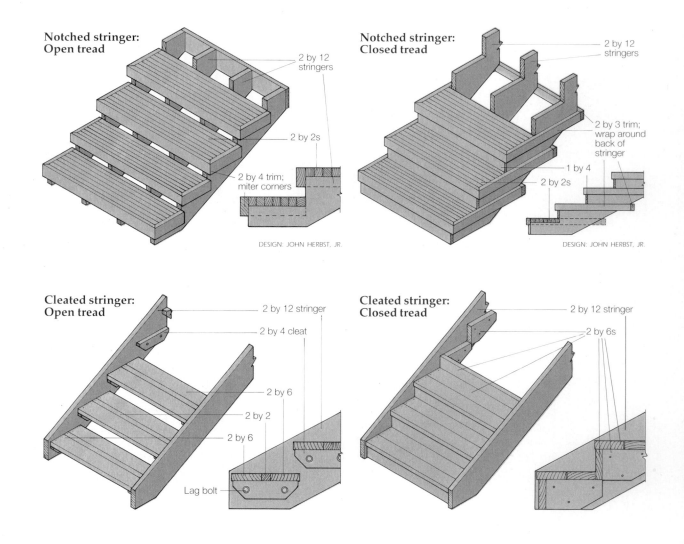

Notched stringer: Open tread
- 2 by 12 stringers
- 2 by 2s
- 2 by 4 trim; miter corners

DESIGN: JOHN HERBST, JR.

Notched stringer: Closed tread
- 2 by 12 stringers
- 2 by 3 trim; wrap around back of stringer
- 1 by 4
- 2 by 2s

DESIGN: JOHN HERBST, JR.

Cleated stringer: Open tread
- 2 by 12 stringer
- 2 by 4 cleat
- 2 by 6
- 2 by 2
- 2 by 6
- Lag bolt

Cleated stringer: Closed tread
- 2 by 12 stringer
- 2 by 6s

basic approaches to construction: stringers with tread cutouts; stringers with cleats; cantilevered steps; overlapping pads (each pad a "minideck"); and construction timbers set into the earth. The illustrations below show each type.

Handrails. In many cases, these are optional. Local codes specify conditions under which they are required. The need for handrails is primarily a safety consideration, but their presence can be psychologically reassuring, even for a low-risk ascent. You may be able to dispense with handrails when steps are 8 feet wide or more, or when the elevation change is only two or three steps. But if stairs are narrower or the elevation change is greater, you may want a handrail even if it is not specified by local code.

The simplest handrail is a single diagonal member that runs parallel to the stair's angle of ascent. The most comfortable height range (common to most code requirements) is 30 to 34 inches measured vertically from the front edge of the tread to the top of the railing. If your deck is surrounded by a decorative railing, you can continue its motif in designing the stair's handrail.

Ramps. Designing steps for a comfortable climb may be a consideration, but in a ramp, ease of ascent is critical. Whether you're negotiating a wheelchair or a wheelbarrow, you *must* be able to "make the grade" without stress.

A ramp's slope is measured in inches of vertical rise per foot of linear distance—the lower rise allowing the easier ascent. For wheelchair access,

construct a ramp with a slope no greater than 1 in 12; for a utility ramp, 1 in 8 will do.

As in step design, the length of the run is part of what makes climbing a ramp pleasant or threatening. In designing a "user-friendly" ramp, be sure that no straight run makes an elevation change greater than 36 inches. For a higher rise, break the run with a level landing where the user can pause. Try to allow for some change in direction (you needn't have dramatic switchbacks) at each landing.

To build a ramp, begin by constructing your deck as though you were going to build stairs. But instead of stairs, you will build a narrow deck (minimum width for wheelchairs is 36 inches) on an incline. Use stringers that are not notched, and run decking crosswise. Be sure to check local codes to see if a handrail is required.

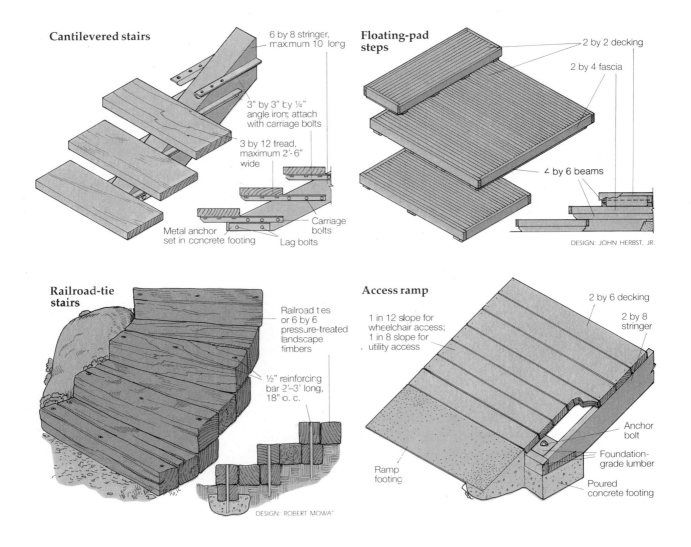

Cantilevered stairs

6 by 8 stringer, maximum 10' long

3" by 3" by ¼" angle iron; attach with carriage bolts

3 by 12 tread, maximum 2'-6" wide

Metal anchor set in concrete footing

Carriage bolts

Lag bolts

Floating-pad steps

2 by 2 decking

2 by 4 fascia

4 by 6 beams

DESIGN: JOHN HERBST, JR.

Railroad-tie stairs

Railroad ties or 6 by 6 pressure-treated landscape timbers

½" reinforcing bar 2'-3' long, 18" o. c.

DESIGN: ROBERT MOWAT

Access ramp

1 in 12 slope for wheelchair access; 1 in 8 slope for utility access

Ramp footing

2 by 6 decking

2 by 8 stringer

Anchor bolt

Foundation-grade lumber

Poured concrete footing

BENCHES

One or more benches gives a deck a finished quality as well as a welcoming look. And a well-designed bench can serve more than one purpose. A perimeter bench with a back can double as a railing; a bench placed somewhere within the deck can become a traffic diverter; and an extra-wide bench can also be used as a low table, perhaps for entertaining, for children's play, or for displaying choice container plants.

In designing benches for your deck, take cues from the railings, screens, even the deck's surface pattern. Such planning achieves an integrated design. But if you want your bench to stand out and serve as a focal point in your garden, you can give free rein to your ingenuity; see, for example, the bird-motif bench at the bottom of this page: the design of its backrest honors the magnificent hawks frequently seen from the owner's property.

Observing a few standards can assure you of a comfortable bench. The seat should be 15 to 18 inches above the deck, and at least 15 inches deep. For an inclined back, you'll find the most comfortable angle is 20° to 30° from vertical.

You can construct benches so that they are an integral part of your deck, build them independently and then attach them when completed, or leave them unattached and movable (but sturdy enough not to topple).

As illustrated on the facing page, built-in benches can be connected to posts extended from the deck's foundation or to vertical members bolted to joists. These uprights can form pedestal supports for bench seats, or become the frame for a bench's back. It's essential that you plan for built-in benches when you design your deck's substructure.

If you build a freestanding bench but want to attach it firmly to the deck later, use brackets or cleats.

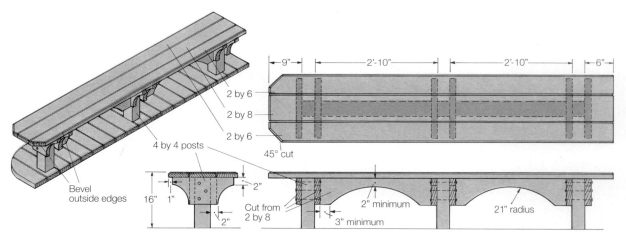

DESIGN: GENE KUNIT

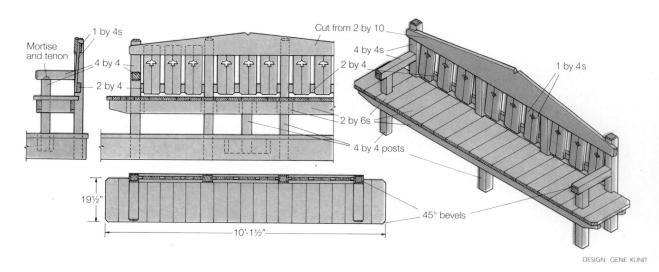

DESIGN: GENE KUNIT

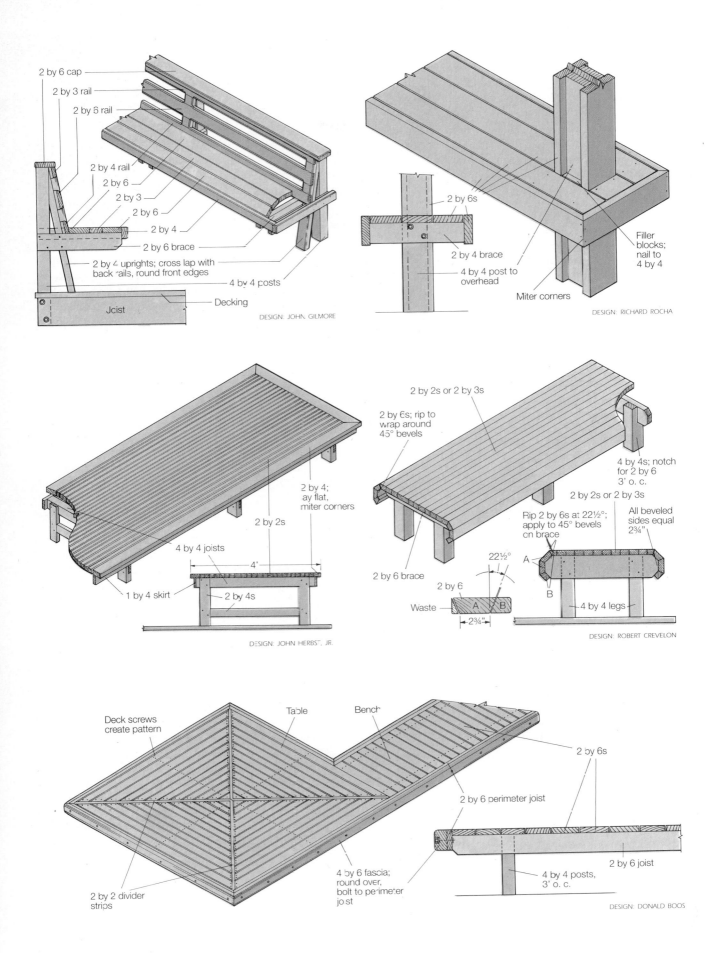

2 by 6 cap
2 by 3 rail
2 by 6 rail
2 by 4 rail
2 by 6
2 by 3
2 by 6
2 by 4
2 by 6 brace
2 by 2 uprights; cross lap with
back rails, round front edges
4 by 4 posts
Decking
Joist

DESIGN: JOHN GILMORE

2 by 6s
2 by 4 brace
4 by 4 post to
overhead
Miter corners
Filler
blocks;
nail to
4 by 4

DESIGN: RICHARD ROCHA

2 by 4;
lay flat,
miter corners
2 by 2s
4 by 4 joists
4'
1 by 4 skirt
2 by 4s

DESIGN: JOHN HERBST, JR.

2 by 2s or 2 by 3s
2 by 6s; rip to
wrap around
45° bevels
4 by 4s; notch
for 2 by 6
3' o. c.
2 by 2s or 2 by 3s
All beveled
sides equal
2¾"
Rip 2 by 6s at 22½°;
apply to 45° bevels
on brace
22½°
A
2 by 6 brace
2 by 6
A   B
B
Waste
2¾"
4 by 4 legs

DESIGN: ROBERT CREVELON

Deck screws
create pattern
Table
Bench
2 by 6s
2 by 6 perimeter joist
2 by 6 joist
4 by 6 fascia;
round over,
bolt to perimeter
joist
4 by 4 posts,
3' o. c.
2 by 2 divider
strips

DESIGN: DONALD BOOS

PLANTERS

To help soften the look of a deck and unite it with the adjacent garden, you'll want to bring some greenery onto it Even if there's no garden nearby, planters let you introduce welcome bits of nature.

Most planters are variations on the basic box. Yet there are seemingly infinite ways to vary the surface ornamentation. No matter what design you devise, you should follow these construction guidelines.

■ Use decay-resistant wood. Redwood and cedar top the list. You also can use wood that is pressure-treated or treated with a copper-based preservative (but do *not* use lumber treated with creosote, which is toxic to plants). If a design calls for plywood, use an exterior grade and treat with preservative all surfaces that will be in contact with soil.

■ When designing a planter entirely of dimensioned lumber, use boards that are nominally 2 inches thick (actual thickness is 1½ inches) for all but small planters.

■ To avoid unsightly rust stains on a finished planter, use nails, screws, or bolts that are galvanized or made of aluminum. For additional sturdiness, use waterproof glue at all corner joints.

■ Make drainage holes in the bottom of each planter. For bottomless planters, just anchor the four corner braces down into the soil.

To give your custom-crafted planter the longest possible life, line its interior with a waterproof barrier to separate wood from soil. Two easy-to-use materials are heavy-duty plastic sheeting and roofing felt (tar paper). Completely cover the bottom and sides, staple the material in place around the top margin (soil will hold the rest snug to the sides), then make slits above the planter's drainage holes. You also could paint the planter's interior with a waterproof, bituminous coating. For longest-lasting protection, have a liner fabricated to fit the planter's inside dimensions—galvanized steel from a

sheet metal shop or vinyl from a waterbed manufacturer. Remember to specify drainage holes.

Because you will be watering the plants in your containers, you should take a few precautions to safeguard your deck from decay. Always provide air space between planter and decking by setting the planters on ½-inch-high decay-resistant spacers. If possible, avoid placing planters over the deck's supporting members; ongoing drainage could lead to structural rot in areas that will be difficult to replace later on.

If you plan to install drip irrigation, you can easily conceal the tubing. Place the main feeder line beneath the deck, then run spaghetti tubing to each container through the deck, between boards, extending it up through a drainage hole in each planter to the soil surface.

For a roof deck, consider building the decking in modules so you can lift them, a section at a time, to make any necessary adjustments to your drip system.

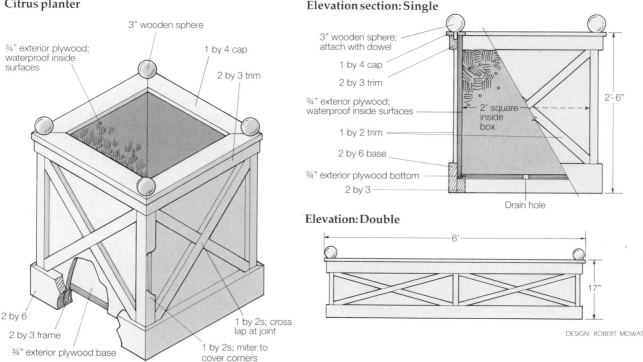

Citrus planter

3" wooden sphere

¾" exterior plywood; waterproof inside surfaces

1 by 4 cap

2 by 3 trim

2 by 6

2 by 3 frame

¾" exterior plywood base

1 by 2s; miter to cover corners

1 by 2s; cross lap at joint

Elevation section: Single

3" wooden sphere; attach with dowel

1 by 4 cap

2 by 3 trim

¾" exterior plywood; waterproof inside surfaces

1 by 2 trim

2 by 6 base

¾" exterior plywood bottom

2 by 3

2' square inside box

2'-6"

Drain hole

Elevation: Double

6'

17'

DESIGN: ROBERT MOWAT

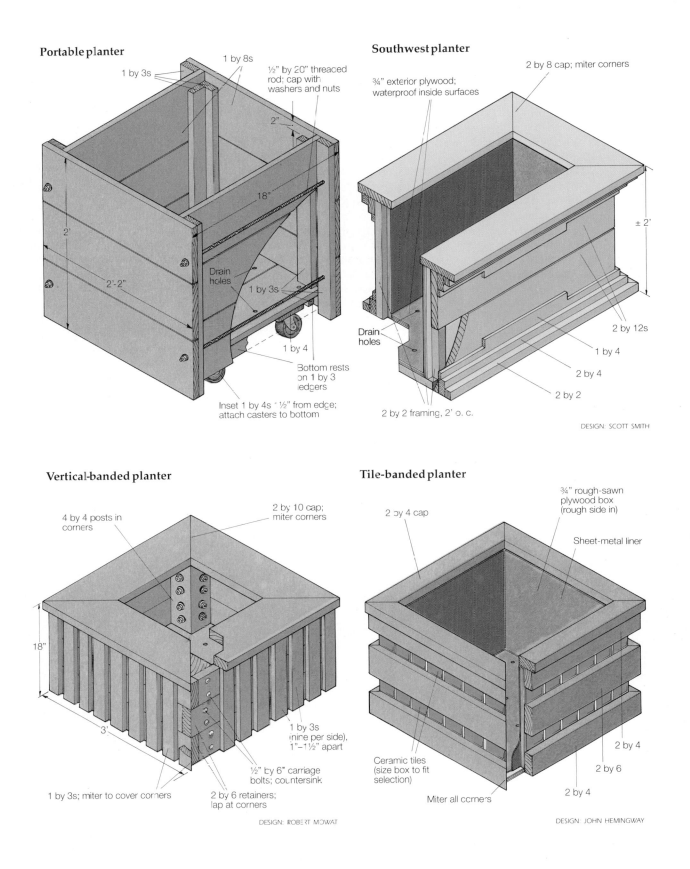

Portable planter

1 by 3s

1 by 8s

½" by 20" threaded rod; cap with washers and nuts

2"

18"

2'

2'-2"

Drain holes

1 by 3s

1 by 4

Bottom rests on 1 by 3 ledgers

Inset 1 by 4s 1½" from edge; attach casters to bottom

Southwest planter

¾" exterior plywood; waterproof inside surfaces

2 by 8 cap; miter corners

± 2'

Drain holes

2 by 12s

1 by 4

2 by 4

2 by 2

2 by 2 framing, 2' o. c.

DESIGN: SCOTT SMITH

Vertical-banded planter

4 by 4 posts in corners

2 by 10 cap; miter corners

18"

3'

1 by 3s (nine per side), 1"–1½" apart

1 by 3s; miter to cover corners

½" by 6" carriage bolts; countersink

2 by 6 retainers; lap at corners

DESIGN: ROBERT MOWAT

Tile-banded planter

2 by 4 cap

¾" rough-sawn plywood box (rough side in)

Sheet-metal liner

Ceramic tiles (size box to fit selection)

Miter all corners

2 by 4

2 by 6

2 by 4

DESIGN: JOHN HEMINGWAY

OVERHEADS

Sometimes the difference between a deck that's inviting and one that's seldom used is nothing more than an overhead structure. The suggestion of a roof can transform an open space into a cozy enclosure. And the relatively simple addition of an overhead, especially one attached to your house, gives you an outdoor "room" to use on fair-weather days.

Of course, there are also purely practical reasons for installing an overhead: to ensure sun control and provide privacy. Depending on its design, an overhead can cast varying degrees of shade, cooling a hot deck and perhaps increasing the number of days it can be used. An overhead can also create instant privacy where none existed—especially significant if the upper-story windows from a neighboring house overlook your deck.

Following a few simple rules will help you plan a satisfying overhead structure. First, coordinate the overhead's design with the style of your house; if your house is without distinct architectural style, the simplest structure generally will look best. Select materials that are compatible with those used in your house and other nearby structures. And before you plan construction, check zoning ordinances as well as building codes for possible restrictions.

Be careful not to create more shade than you really want. An overhead in a shady north-facing location should be kept as light and open as possible. It helps to know the sun's path through the sky in your locale so you can judge when and at what angle the sun will strike your overhead at different times of year.

You'll also want to be sure your overhead doesn't block desirable views, such as distant mountain tops, from the deck beneath or from inside the house.

Most overheads begin with simple post-and-beam construction. An overhead attached to an existing structure may spring from a ledger, but it needs a post-and-beam system for perimeter support. Additional lattice-like layers of successively smaller lumber may be added in alternating directions. Note that a *notched* joist-and-beam connection is adequate for supporting light and airy vines, but not for holding dense foliage or additional members of heavy lumber.

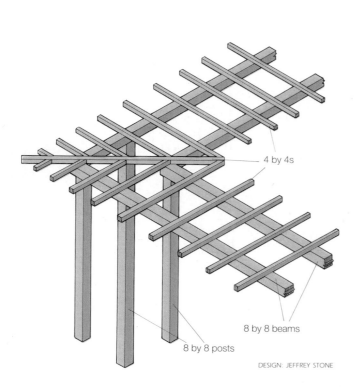

4 by 4s

8 by 8 beams

8 by 8 posts

DESIGN: JEFFREY STONE

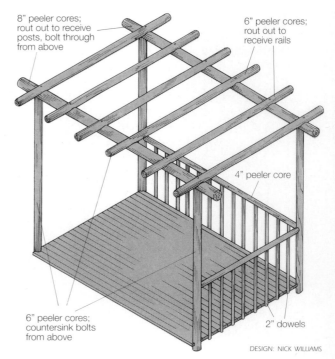

8" peeler cores; rout out to receive posts, bolt through from above

6" peeler cores; rout out to receive rails

4" peeler core

6" peeler cores; countersink bolts from above

2" dowels

DESIGN: NICK WILLIAMS

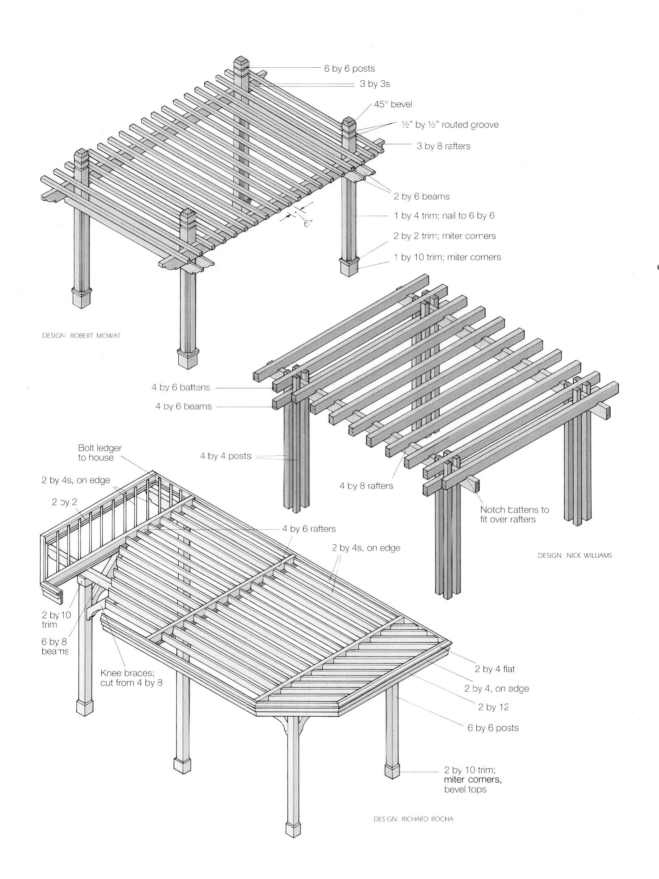

6 by 6 posts

3 by 3s

45° bevel

½" by ½" routed groove

3 by 8 rafters

2 by 6 beams

1 by 4 trim; nail to 6 by 6

2 by 2 trim; miter corners

1 by 10 trim; miter corners

6"

DESIGN: ROBERT MOWAT

4 by 6 battens

4 by 6 beams

4 by 4 posts

4 by 8 rafters

Notch battens to
fit over rafters

DESIGN: NICK WILLIAMS

Bolt ledger
to house

2 by 4s, on edge

2 by 2

4 by 6 rafters

2 by 4s, on edge

2 by 10
trim

6 by 8
beams

Knee braces;
cut from 4 by 8

2 by 4 flat

2 by 4, on edge

2 by 12

6 by 6 posts

2 by 10 trim;
miter corners,
bevel tops

DESIGN: RICHARD ROCHA

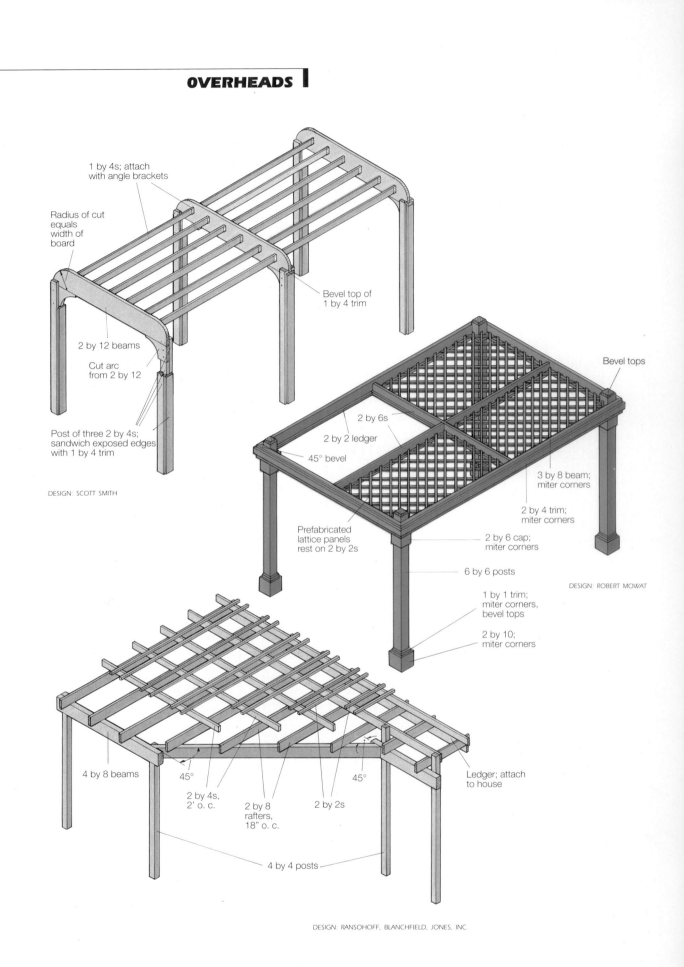

1 by 4s; attach with angle brackets

Radius of cut equals width of board

Bevel top of 1 by 4 trim

2 by 12 beams

Cut arc from 2 by 12

Post of three 2 by 4s; sandwich exposed edges with 1 by 4 trim

DESIGN: SCOTT SMITH

Bevel tops

2 by 6s

2 by 2 ledger

45° bevel

3 by 8 beam; miter corners

2 by 4 trim; miter corners

2 by 6 cap; miter corners

Prefabricated lattice panels rest on 2 by 2s

6 by 6 posts

DESIGN: ROBERT MOWAT

1 by 1 trim; miter corners, bevel tops

2 by 10; miter corners

4 by 8 beams

45°

2 by 4s, 2' o. c.

2 by 8 rafters, 18" o. c.

2 by 2s

45°

Ledger; attach to house

4 by 4 posts

DESIGN: RANSOHOFF, BLANCHFIELD, JONES, INC.

DECKS AS BRIDGES

In the simplest terms, a bridge is an elevated walkway that allows traffic between two points on either side of an otherwise difficult passage.

Although the bridge illustrated below crosses a terraced ravine between deck and garden, the same sort of bridge could be built to connect two separate elevated decks, to span a garden pond or stream, or simply to allow easy passage over rough or irregular terrain.

Your bridge will need these four components: firm anchorage at each end; sturdy beams to traverse the span; flooring (decking); and railings.

The bridge illustrated below shows a basic type of anchorage. Because it was designed to cross a garden gully, it required the use of a concrete footing. Spanning the gully are three 4 by 12 beams; but in their place, six equally spaced 2 by 12s could have been used.

Construction methods will vary according to the site: some settings call for poured concrete footings, while other spans may be accomplished with another basic type of anchorage, post-and-beam construction. Choice of railing designs is considerable (see pages 76–78). With additional joists or blocking, you can even vary decking patterns. Be very sure to develop bridge plans in accordance with local building codes.

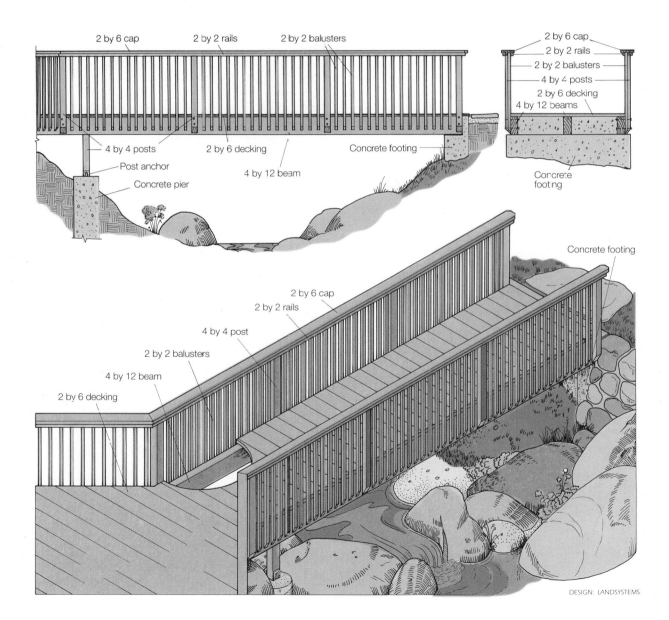

2 by 6 cap • 2 by 2 rails • 2 by 2 balusters • 4 by 4 posts • 2 by 6 decking • Post anchor • Concrete pier • 2 by 6 decking • 4 by 12 beam • Concrete footing

2 by 6 cap • 2 by 2 rails • 2 by 2 balusters • 4 by 4 posts • 2 by 6 decking • 4 by 12 beams • Concrete footing

2 by 6 cap • 2 by 2 rails • 4 by 4 post • 2 by 2 balusters • 4 by 12 beam • 2 by 6 decking • Concrete footing

DESIGN: LANDSYSTEMS

ENGAWAS

The Japanese *engawa*, or "wraparound deck," is simply a walkway or platform that extends the interior floor level out to or beyond the house's eaves. Particularly where windows drop to the floor, an adjacent engawa expands a room visually, while providing a subtle but harmonious transition to the landscape.

In practical terms, an engawa can serve three useful purposes. If its length abuts more than one room, it can form an exterior hallway. Typically set one step above ground level, the engawa can serve as a single broad step. And here as in Japan, the engawa can become a display platform to set off choice container plants or art objects.

Build an engawa as you would an attached deck. Secure a ledger along the house wall to form support on one side. Short beams from the ledger to pier blocks work as the cross-members, and decking is laid parallel to the house wall. Matching decking boards to interior flooring size and direction enhances the indoor-outdoor connection. A fascia run across the beam ends gives the outside edge a finished look.

If the engawa extends beyond the eaves, install gutters to divert runoff from the roof. Some eaves can be extended, as illustrated. To lengthen rafters, sandwich them with same-size lumber bolted to the rafters.

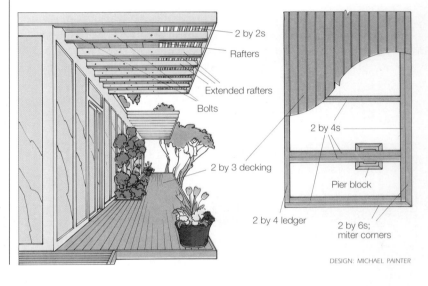

2 by 2s
Rafters
Extended rafters
Bolts
2 by 3 decking
2 by 4 ledger
2 by 4s
Pier block
2 by 6s; miter corners

DESIGN: MICHAEL PAINTER

LIGHTS

Not only will strategically placed lighting have great aesthetic value (whether you use the deck after dark or merely view it from the house), it can also make dark steps and shadowy passageways safer.

Our illustrations show typical situations where outdoor lighting adds a finishing touch: along a pathway, beside steps, under a railing or bench, and in an overhead structure.

Assess your lighting needs before you surface your deck. Some areas may be difficult or impossible to reach later.

Installing low-voltage outdoor lighting is a simple and safe weekend project. You can buy kits that contain all materials you'll need for a specified number of lights. The wiring may remain on the surface or be slightly buried; no permit is required.

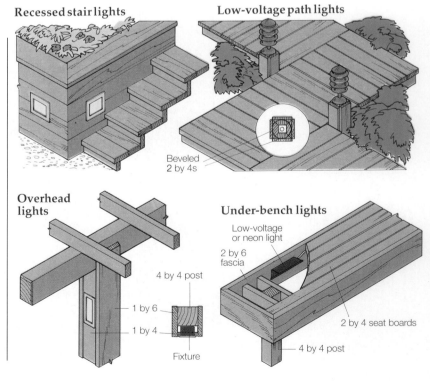

Recessed stair lights

Low-voltage path lights

Beveled 2 by 4s

Overhead lights

4 by 4 post

1 by 6

1 by 4

Fixture

Under-bench lights

Low-voltage or neon light

2 by 6 fascia

2 by 4 seat boards

4 by 4 post

TABLES

If you plan to use your deck for outdoor entertaining, you'll find that a table will be an essential addition. You can, of course, purchase ready-made tables. However, if you prefer one that is custom-tailored to your deck and its other amenities, you will want to build the table yourself.

The simplest tables, as shown, are constructed like four-legged backless benches (see pages 84–85). You can also choose a double-pedestal style. Plan the table's height to suit its intended purpose: 16 to 18 inches for a coffee table or childrens' play surface, 28 inches for dining or games.

We also show a table that is slightly more elaborate. This is a variation on the traditional four-legged style. It was designed to fit into a specific conversation nook.

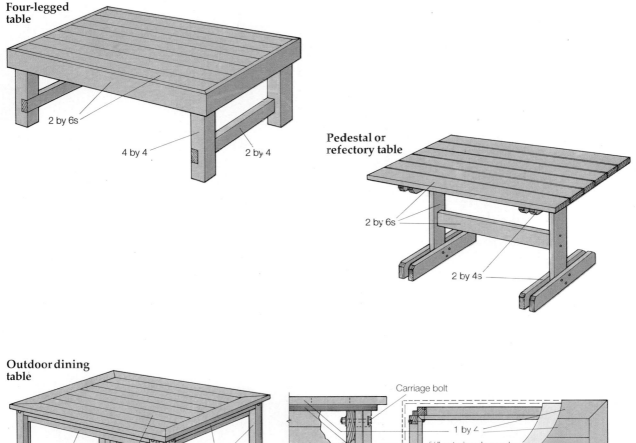

Four-legged table

2 by 6s

4 by 4

2 by 4

Pedestal or refectory table

2 by 6s

2 by 4s

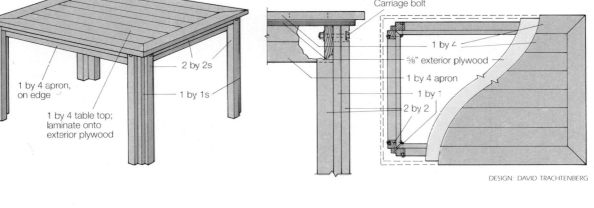

Outdoor dining table

1 by 4 apron, on edge

1 by 4 table top; laminate onto exterior plywood

2 by 2s

1 by 1s

Carriage bolt

1 by 4

⅝" exterior plywood

1 by 4 apron

1 by 1

2 by 2

DESIGN: DAVID TRACHTENBERG

SPECIAL UNITS

Many other built-in amenities can enhance your deck's usefulness. Some, like the storage bench or the hidden sandbox, combine a second feature with the primary one, allowing one space to perform double duty. Others, like the custom-crafted barbecue unit and the multifunction serving bar, lend specific new dimensions to a deck's entertainment potential.

You can adapt the drawings of these four projects for use in your own situation. But let these special unit ideas stimulate your imagination as well: they may inspire new design avenues of your own that will make your deck more useful, pleasing, and individual.

HIDDEN SANDBOX

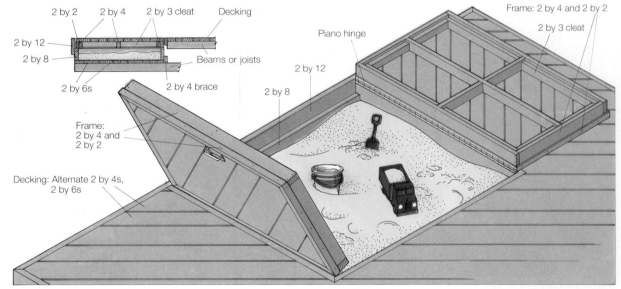

2 by 2   2 by 4   2 by 3 cleat   Decking

2 by 12
2 by 8

2 by 6s   2 by 4 brace

Frame:
2 by 4 and
2 by 2

Decking: Alternate 2 by 4s,
2 by 6s

Beams or joists

Piano hinge

2 by 12

2 by 8

Frame: 2 by 4 and 2 by 2

2 by 3 cleat

BENCH STORAGE

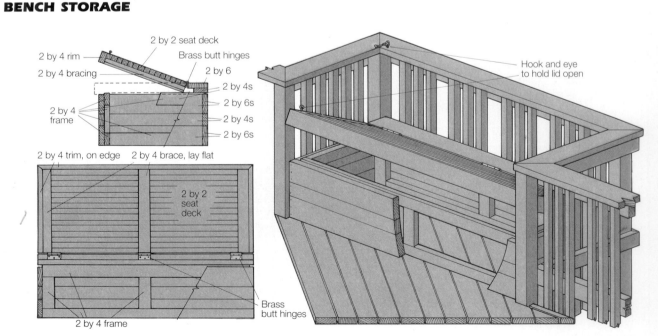

2 by 4 rim

2 by 4 bracing

2 by 4
frame

2 by 2 seat deck

Brass butt hinges

2 by 6

2 by 4s

2 by 6s

2 by 4s

2 by 6s

2 by 4 trim, on edge   2 by 4 brace, lay flat

2 by 2
seat
deck

2 by 4 frame

Brass
butt hinges

Hook and eye
to hold lid open

BARBECUE

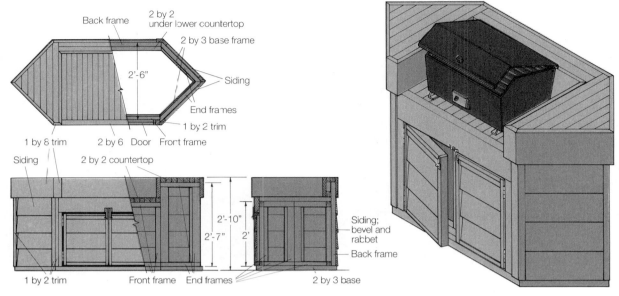

Back frame
2 by 2 under lower countertop
2 by 3 base frame
Siding
2'-6"
End frames
1 by 2 trim
1 by 8 trim
2 by 6   Door   Front frame
Siding
2 by 2 countertop
2'-10"
2'-7"
2'
Siding; bevel and rabbet
Back frame
1 by 2 trim
Front frame   End frames
2 by 3 base

DESIGN: ROBERT CREVELON

ENTERTAINMENT CENTER

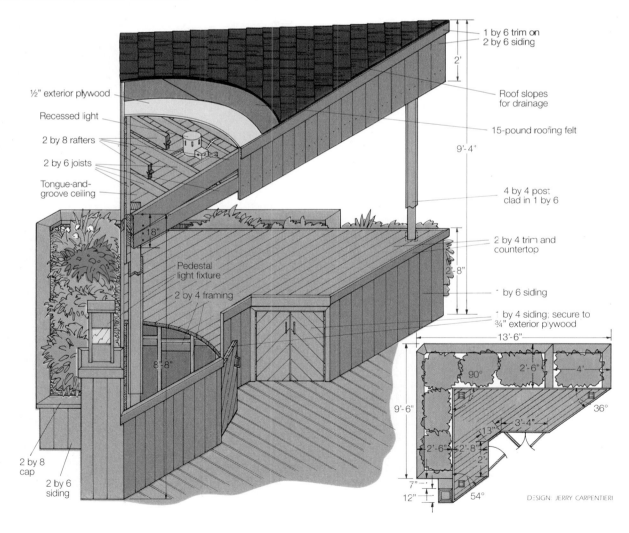

½" exterior plywood
Recessed light
2 by 8 rafters
2 by 6 joists
Tongue-and-groove ceiling

1 by 6 trim on 2 by 6 siding
2'
Roof slopes for drainage
15-pound roofing felt
9'-4"
4 by 4 post clad in 1 by 6
2 by 4 trim and countertop
2'-8"
1 by 6 siding
1 by 4 siding; secure to ¾" exterior plywood

18"
Pedestal light fixture
2 by 4 framing
8'-8"

2 by 8 cap
2 by 6 siding

13'-6"
9'-6"
90°   2'-6"   4'
36°
13"   3'-4"
2'-6"   2'-8"
2'
7"
12"   54°

DESIGN: JERRY CARPENTIERI

INDEX